S0-BXD-743

# TIPS FOR RAISING TEENS
## A Primer for Parents

Robert J. McCarty

PAULIST PRESS
New York • Mahwah, N.J.

Copyright © 1998 by Robert J. McCarty

All rights reserved. No part of this book may be reproduced or transmitted in any form or by any means, electronic or mechanical, including photocopying, recording or by any information storage and retrieval system without permission in writing from the Publisher.

LIBRARY OF CONGRESS CATALOGING-IN-PUBLICATION DATA

McCarty, Robert J.
    Tips for raising teens : a primer for parents / Robert J. McCarty.
        p.   cm.
    ISBN 0-8091-3818-2 (alk. paper)
    1. Parent and teenager.  2. Parenting.  3. Adolescent psychology.
4. Parenting—Religious aspects—Christianity. I. Title.
HQ799.15.M32    1998
649′.125—dc21                                                      98-21716
                                                                          CIP


Cover design by Moe Berman
Interior design by Joseph E. Petta
Typeset in 11/13 Baskerville

Published by Paulist Press
997 Macarthur Boulevard
Mahwah, New Jersey 07430

www.paulistpress.com

Printed and bound in the
United States of America

# Contents

# Introduction

The following statement reflects the thoughts of many of today's parents concerned about their teenagers.

> If I can just get my kids through high school without their doing drugs, getting pregnant, getting hurt or getting into trouble...and if I could only get them to go to church...then I will be satisfied!

With all the pressures and problems of our society today, many parents believe that these hopes are the most desirable and realistic goals for raising children. We all know enough young people who have been victims of any or all of the above situations to make these beliefs well founded. However, I am not ready to settle for just these goals for young people. I have worked too long with young people to believe that if they are drug-free, safe, chaste, and church-going, that is all we can expect from them. These qualities are certainly important, but there is so much more in our teenagers. Teenagers bring an energy, an idealism, and a passion for living that is a gift to the adult world today. Young people have a compassion and a hunger for justice that demands opportunity for expression. Lowering parental expectations of their children is not the solution. Having realistic expectations, even while parents call their children to something more in their lives, will ultimately better prepare their children for a healthy, happy, and mature adulthood.

Most of us who are parents do want something more for our children. The plethora of books and videos on raising children and the number of parents involved in their children's schools, community organizations, and sports, dance, and music programs reflect the concern of so many parents. You are among those! Your willingness to simply pick up this book is a sign of your concern. You want to know more in order to be a better parent. However, your love and concern for your children are more important and will have more impact on how you parent than any book ever could.

The need for another book on parenting is arguable. However, my experience working with teenagers and their families over the past twenty-five years has led me to believe that we could all benefit from a book on parenting teenagers that is simple, clear, and user-friendly. As one who has parented for twenty-three years—my own daughter and various other young people who have come to live in my home—I know I have always looked for another new insight or another angle which would help me better understand my own daughter and all the other young people with whom I have been blessed to work.

Effective parenting is concerned with the whole young person, responding to his or her physical, emotional, psychological, and spiritual needs. An important focus of this book is assisting parents in meeting their teenagers' spiritual needs and fostering their growth in faith. Our children's faith development as adolescents is integral to the kind of adults they will become and the kind of life they will live.

This dimension of parenting is very rewarding, even with the challenge of being a faith-filled person in a sometimes hostile secular world.

This book does not pretend to have all the answers. There will always be a need for new insights on the parenting of teenagers as the situations confronting teens and families change. Our society is already witness to myriad configurations of family makeup. Families are two-parent, single-parent, step-parent, blended, and multi-generational. Sometimes family membership differs from midweek to weekend. The uniqueness of our family situations makes parenting all the more challenging and highlights the need for approaches, techniques, and strategies which enhance the relationship between parents and their teenage children.

Not only can we survive our children's adolescent years, but we can enjoy, appreciate, and even cherish these years of intense growth, new insights, boundless energy, and excitement. This book, therefore, is written for the benefit of parents and children both, because children need us to be the best parents possible. Children need parental help, guidance, support, and nurturing as they move through their adolescent years, especially in a time and in a world where so many harmful and destructive experiences confront them.

The following chapters have been arranged in this manner: chapter 1 addresses the situation of young people today; chapter 2 describes the psychological and developmental tasks of young people; chapter 3 offers some practical suggestions for improving parent–teen relationships; chapter 4 discusses the concept of self-esteem and provides practical strategies for enhancing self-esteem in our teenagers; chapter 5 examines the process of faith development in young people and provides suggestions for fostering the faith of our teenagers.

The Appendix provides activities and sharing exercises

which parents and teens can do together as a way of fostering understanding and communication.

Although the temptation is to skip right to the practical strategies in chapters 3, 4, and 5, a more worthwhile approach is reading the chapters sequentially. The strategies will make more sense if the reader first has an understanding of the context of young people: their situation today and their developmental tasks. So, on with the task and challenge of surviving and thriving with teenagers!

# 1 · The Situation of Young People Today

See if the following words seem to describe any teenager you know:

> Our youth love luxury; they have bad manners; contempt for authority; they show disrespect for elders and love chatter in place of exercise. Children are now tyrants, not the servants of their households. They no longer rise when elders enter the room. They contradict their parents, chatter before company, gobble up their food and tyrannize their teachers.

This quotation is ascribed to Socrates (470–399 B.C.E.). Or consider this comment:

> I see no hope for the future of our people if they are dependent on the frivolous youth of today, for certainly all youth are reckless beyond words. When I was young, we were taught to be discreet and respectful of elders, but the present youth are exceedingly wise and impatient of restraint.
>
> Hesiod, 800 B.C.E.

# 6 TIPS FOR RAISING TEENS

And finally:

> The young people of today think of nothing but themselves.
> They have no reverence for parents or old age; they are
> impatient of all restraint; they talk as if they alone know
> everything and what passes for wisdom in us is foolishness
> in them. As for girls, they are foolish and immodest and
> unwomanly in speech, behavior and dress.
>
> Peter the Hermit, 1083 A.D.

Clearly, some characteristics of children and youth are
timeless and universal. Certain aspects of the experience of
living with children are shared by every culture and society
throughout time. Even scripture tells the story of Jesus wan-
dering away from his parents while on a family trip and
their not finding him for three days. And when they do find
him in the temple, Jesus is very nonplussed and seems
unconcerned for his parents' anxiety. If this had happened
today, Jesus' picture would have been on a milk carton!

Parents do have to keep perspective about some of the
behavioral habits of their children and avoid overreacting.
However, the worlds of Socrates and of Joseph, Mary and
Jesus were very different than the world of young people
today.

## IMPACT OF SOCIETY

Children today are the product of a society and world experiencing rapid change. Advances in media, computers, and
technology are coupled with sociological and political
change. Children are becoming masters of the Internet and
live in an age of instant experiences and virtual reality. Families were absorbed by the bombing of the federal building
in Oklahoma City and even the funerals of Princess Diana
and Mother Teresa.

Adults and children alike watch world events unfold on

TV, as evidenced by the ability to watch the Gulf War, the Balkans' Civil War, and the horror of ethnic cleansing in Rwanda. Families also witness the violence that seems to be escalating in cities, towns, and neighborhoods across the country every time they watch the television news broadcast. Global and local issues are brought into the family's living room every day and the bad news certainly seems to dominate any good news that might be happening. The concept of "the mean world syndrome" has been coined to denote the perspective of the world created especially through the media that concentrate on the bad news, coloring one's impression of current events and the world in which young people are growing up.

Our parenting styles are greatly influenced by our impression of the current climate in society. We seem to be raising our children to be more careful, even distrustful of the world around them. Parents fear the possibility of their children being physically, sexually, or psychologically abused and so they teach their children to be untrusting of strangers, neighbors, political leaders, and even some religious leaders. Parents see the increase of drug and alcohol use, teen pregnancy, and the spread of AIDS and we try to be ever more vigilant and protective of our children. The world in which today's children are growing up is very different than the world in which their parents grew up. The adage, "When I was their age," is itself outmoded, for we were never "their age," not in the sense of trying to come to maturity in a society that seems as threatening and unsupportive as the current situation.

And recent statistics support this perception. According to the Children's Defense Fund, which keeps accurate and current statistics on the situation of children and youth in society, the following happens every day in the United States. Collated in 1997 and titled, "One Day in the Lives of

America's Children," these statistics paint a very painful reality. Every day:

| | |
|---:|:---|
| 2,795 | teenagers get pregnant |
| 1,115 | teenagers have abortions |
| 1,420 | teenagers give birth |
| 27 | children die from poverty |
| 3 | children die from child abuse |
| 16 | children die from guns |
| 30 | children are wounded by guns |
| 135,000 | children bring guns to school |
| 18 | youth and young adults commit suicide |
| 8,400 | teenagers become sexually active |
| 5,702 | children are arrested |
| 3,356 | teenagers drop out of school |
| 8,523 | children are abused or neglected |
| 1,234 | children run away from home |
| 2,860 | children see their parents divorced |
| 100,000 | children are homeless |

Indeed, we have every reason to be concerned about our children. Parents are afraid that their children will be hurt physically, sexually, emotionally, or spiritually. Every time our children walk out our doors, we ought to be saying a prayer for their safety. No longer are our children's schools the safe havens we always assumed they would be. Parents don't send their children to their playgrounds without supervision. For some children, even their own neighborhood streets aren't safe. Parents have become more careful about allowing their children to stay overnight at the homes of their friends, rightfully calling to check with the parents.

Children and teenagers have so many important decisions to make, so many factors weighing on them, so many opportunities for things to go wrong, it's a wonder that so many young people turn out OK. And, in fact, many young people do avoid the myriad pitfalls that seem to characterize adolescence. The high school graduation rate is the highest in our country's history. Teenagers contributed 2.1 billion hours of service to their communities in 1995. Two million teenagers participated in National Service Day on April 25, 1995. Many become healthy and happy adults (just look at us!), and so many young people do love their parents. Clearly, despite the statistics, many young people are surviving and even thriving. Why? Because they want to! Young people have a hunger to succeed in life. They want to be happy, to get along with their parents, to have worthwhile occupations, and to be able to find meaning and make sense out of life. And in order to support young people, parents and the rest of society have to pay more attention to these hungers.

## HUNGERS OF YOUNG PEOPLE

The following description of the hungers of young people comes from the experience of those involved in Catholic youth ministry. However, these hungers are generic to all young people, in all denominations and faiths. They may be expressed through a variety of behaviors, attitudes, and values, and in a language that is particular to a certain age group in a certain area of the country. But the experience of these hungers seems to be very characteristic of young people growing up in our society today.

## THE HUNGER FOR MEANING AND PURPOSE

Perhaps the great fear of young people today is that things don't matter, that there is no real meaning and purpose to their lives, their relationships, their future, their education or possible occupation. They look around society and see the quest for more possessions, wealth, and power, and many young people wonder if that's all there is to life. Many youth are concerned about their future, wondering what kind of world will exist for them, what opportunities will be available, and whether they will be happy. Older teens ask questions about their place in this world and grow anxious about the type of occupation or vocation they will have.

Young people hunger for a sense of meaning and purpose. They don't want to just go through life, they want to have an impact, they want to make a difference. In their youthful optimism, unscathed by the skepticism of many adults, teens are looking for something that provides meaning and value. Faith and a relationship with God should respond to this hunger by calling youth "to the fullness of their humanity, centered in God and expressed in the love of others."

## THE HUNGER FOR CONNECTION

Beginning with their experience of their family, young people express a need for belonging and connection on a variety of levels. Younger adolescents, generally those youth between ten and fifteen years old, are joiners, seeking out clubs, scouting, sports teams, and even gangs. The peer group and friends provide a sense of connection outside the home, even while, as older adolescents, they come to see themselves as connected to the larger communities of school, church, and society. Young people want a place where they fit in, where they are valued, where they are welcomed and accepted, and where "everyone knows their name."

## THE HUNGER FOR RECOGNITION

Young people hunger for the affirmation that they are OK. Regardless of how secure they may seem outwardly, they want and need to feel worthwhile and important. They need to know that they have gifts and talents to share with others. Young people want to feel loved and appreciated, especially by their parents and other significant adults. Integral to this hunger for recognition is their need to be listened to, affirming that they have something valuable to say. Young people are crying out for genuine, positive attention.

## THE HUNGER FOR JUSTICE

Teenagers have an innate sense of justice. Though the earliest expression of this might sound hollow to parents who remember, "That's not fair," the desire for justice, equality, and peace is very present in teenagers. Teens experience injustice, violence, hatred, prejudice, and even poverty— poverty of possessions and/or the spirit. They want to imagine a world where everyone has equal access to the goods and resources necessary to meet basic needs. Many are quick to volunteer their time, energy, and talents on behalf of the less fortunate. They see the ills of society and they hunger to make things right.

## THE HUNGER FOR THE HOLY

Many young people today are searching for an authentic experience of God. They see the gap between professed belief and lived practice in their church communities, and they criticize the apparent hypocrisy. "Young people are searching for a faith that makes sense, that provides direction and meaning, and that challenges." They want a religion that helps them understand their experience of life with its joys and sufferings, as well as enabling them to better articulate their experience of God. And they want to be connected with others who are on this same search.

We as parents and the rest of society have to address these hungers in order to really foster the personal and spiritual growth of our teenagers and assist them in their journey toward healthy, happy, and holy adulthood. The failure to do so will cause our teens to go elsewhere in order to feed their hungers. Parents have to honestly acknowledge the power of cults, gangs, and other groupings to attract young people, in addition to the allure of risky behaviors such as drinking, drug use, inappropriate sexual relations, and crime.

Young people experience these hungers today as they simultaneously grow to maturity in their families, in their neighborhoods, and in the larger society. This growth to maturity is an individual process that includes the successful resolution of certain psychological tasks. The next chapter examines these tasks more clearly.

# 2 · Psychological and Developmental Tasks of Young People

This chapter begins with identifying the internal, developmental tasks of adolescence, those tasks that are integral to this stage of psychological growth. The second part of the chapter describes the generation gap that is a natural outcome of the intersecting of adolescence and parents' middlescence, with some suggestions for bridging the gap that can develop between parents and teens.

The adolescence that is often romanticized in song, story, and proverb—"These are the best days of your life"—is a myth. Rare are the parents who would go back and do their teenage years all over again, unless, of course, they could take the wisdom and learnings of their adulthood with them. Perhaps the most accurate definition of this time of life is that adolescence begins around age eleven and goes on until one recovers. The idea of recovering from our adolescence may be closer to the truth of what happens during this period of incredible physical and psychological growth. In a sense many parents may be "recovering adolescents," still coping with some of the turmoil and challenges of their teen years.

During this period of life, certain tasks must be accomplished or worked through. These tasks, often unknown to the teen who is actually experiencing their effect, can be painfully obvious to the observing parent. These internal tasks seem to combine during the teen years to create a time of explosions.


INTERNAL TASKS

Adolescence requires the handling of these five developmental tasks in order to foster healthy psychological development.

- Physical development
- Emotional development
- Developing a personal belief and value system
- Developing healthy relationships
- Developing a sense of individuality and personal identity

These tasks occur simultaneously, causing that much more confusion for the adolescent, and challenging parents to greater sensitivity, understanding, and patience.


*Physical Development*

The first task during adolescence is to develop physically. During the years following the onset of puberty the teen's body literally explodes. Growth spurts are common and often painful. Many of us can remember the experience during our own adolescent years of getting up one morning and looking in the mirror, either with hope or trepidation, to see what had happened to our bodies overnight. Teens can be so afraid of being physically too underdeveloped or overdeveloped, too tall or too short, too heavy or too thin, too different or too much the same as their peers. Their concern is "Am I normal?" And their peers, who are grappling with the same concerns, are their points of comparison! They suffer from uncontrollable voice changes, hoping to sound more mature, but having to live with the sudden volume and tone changes. The onset of acne is probably the most painful sign of the physical changes occurring within their bodies. For many teenagers, acne is the most feared scourge, affecting one's self-image and one's ability to interact with peers. I can remember sitting in high school lamenting this adolescent leprosy and realizing that none of my teachers suffered from acne. That was the first time I allowed myself to believe that perhaps acne was an adolescent issue and that I might grow out of it, though this was little consolation in my immediate world. The problem is that there is no set schedule or pattern for physical development. For some, age twelve seems to kick off the growth spurt, while others are sixteen years old when their bodies change.

I can remember being 5'2"tall from eighth grade into my junior year of high school. I experienced very little or no physical change at a time when my sister, who was two years younger, had already started looking sixteen years old while only thirteen. What an embarrassment to be mistaken for the younger sibling by strangers, teachers, and other teenagers. And at 5'2", with a body unsuited for most sports, I was a fast runner, which was essential for my survival, given my quick, verbal retorts used as a defense mechanism. In retrospect, I know that I compensated for my size with a glib tongue and sarcastic wit that often put me in physical confrontation with my peers. Being able to run fast allowed me to live long enough to make it into my junior year of high school during which I grew seven inches in height. What an experience to have a body that was growing out of control, greatly affecting any sense of coordination. I went from being a fast runner to not being able to walk upstairs without tripping.

## Emotional Development

Simultaneous with these physical explosions, the teen's emotions explode. They experience sudden highs and lows, intense moments of happiness and sadness, and wild mood swings. Learning how to name and express these emotions is the second task of adolescence.

In a parenting workshop a mother of three teenagers recalled her adolescence and described herself as a thirteen year old who had cried her way through the eighth grade. She remembered crying whenever someone spoke to her in the "wrong" tone of voice, and when no one spoke to her at all. And she didn't know why. Parents are often surprised by the intensity of their children's emotional response to suggestions they make about their dress, requests for assistance around the house, or simple inquiries about school or friends. Youth's emotions are worn on their sleeve, ready to just burst out with the smallest provocation. Knowing that our children's emotions are especially volatile during this period of development may help us better understand many of the conflicts and arguments we might have with our children.

I remember having a conversation with my daughter, Shannon, when she was twelve years old. Actually, I thought it was a conversation; she thought it was a fight. I asked her why she was putting so much energy into this issue (long since forgotten), which I thought was fairly inconsequential (not a good attitude for me to have taken!), and she said, "Dad, I'm a pre-teen and I have to start getting ready." I could only surmise that she had either read the book or seen the movie on being a teenager and she was in training. Either way, this was an accurate foreshadowing of years to come.

We have to remember that no matter how illogical the

strength of our children's emotions might seem (emotions aren't logical anyway), these emotions are still very real for them. Anger, love, frustration, happiness, despair, joy, and loneliness are not right or wrong. Emotions are the signals that portray our children's reaction to the surrounding environment of relationships, family, school, peers, and all the other dimensions of their life. A very important task for children, however, is to learn how to express their feelings in appropriate ways. Parents have to allow them to ventilate or share their feelings, and, even more importantly, let them know that it's OK to feel whatever it is they are feeling. But be careful. Even though we may understand how our children are feeling, we can hardly ever say, "I understand how you feel" or "I know just how you feel" or "I remember feeling that way too," because for our children, the intensity of the emotions may be so new to them that they honestly believe that no one could ever really understand how they are feeling, especially their parents. The best strategy for parents is to let their children have their emotions and assist them in naming how they are feeling. Often teens don't yet have the language to name the emotion they are experiencing. Teens and pre-teens will say, "I feel bad," or "I feel OK," not realizing that there are hundreds of descriptive words from which to choose. Naming the feeling is the first step in mastering its expression.

## Developing Personal Beliefs and Values

A third task during adolescence is to develop a personal value and belief system. Prior to adolescence children rely on an inherited value and belief system to provide a sense of meaning and a standard for behavior. Parental values are their values. But during adolescence or even earlier, they become aware that not everyone thinks, acts, or believes the way their family does. Teens are confronted by multiple belief and value systems in school, their playgrounds, on the sports fields, in the media and through television. They enter into an age of questioning and challenging, trying to understand what they believe and why they hold certain values. This is the awakening of their hunger for meaning and purpose as described in chapter 1. They may even experiment with different beliefs and behaviors as they search to find those values that help them make sense of their life and future, and provide a sense of meaning.

This experience can be very fearful for those teens who haven't had an opportunity to discuss their beliefs, to put into words what they believe, or who have never had to defend their beliefs to a challenging peer. Chapter 5 will look specifically at how faith develops during this time of challenging and questioning, especially during adolescence, and the importance of parental and adult modeling.

## *Developing Relationships*

A fourth task for emerging adolescents is developing their relationship skills. When asked, younger adolescents will often claim to have ten, twelve, or more "close" or "best" friends, while older adolescents will usually identify only one, two or maybe three "close" friends. Building upon the friendships of their childhood, adolescents learn how to deepen relationships, experiencing new levels of commitment outside their family, and expanding their capacity for intimacy, resulting in fewer, but deeper friendships. This experience of intimacy, of interpersonal bonding first with peers of the same sex and then with those of the opposite gender, is a critical task since it foreshadows their later permanent, committed relationships like marriage. Within these relationships teens experience a sense of connectedness and belonging outside the family. These friendships are so very important to young people, often causing conflict when the teenager is asked to choose between family and friends. We can sometimes have a difficult time understanding the bonding that occurs between adolescents, and sometimes it's that we just don't remember our own first "real" friends—those early "best friends" that marked our moving outside our family in order to meet our need for intimacy and belonging. This developmental task is enhanced or inaugurated by a teen's exploding (are we getting the hint about adolescent development?) sexuality.

Sexuality is the impetus to intimacy and that gift from God that draws people into relationships with others. Most of us can remember how in the early grades in elementary school the teacher could control behavior with threats of making misbehaving students sit next to the girls or boys—the opposite sex, whichever was the opposite! But somewhere in the later grades, around junior high age, this strategy no longer worked. In fact, sitting with the opposite sex became almost a reward. Suddenly students were forming relationships with peers of the opposite sex and were hanging around in mixed groups. Something had changed. Their sexuality had exploded. Junior high young people are likened to hormones on wheels with this new interest in dating, in their physical appearance, and in the style of clothing they wear. All of this flows from this new impetus to relationships brought on by our developing sexuality.

When this task is considered along with the first task of physical development, the angst and anxiety that accompanies a teen's physical development is very understandable. Suddenly during adolescence children's attention is focused outward toward the world of their peers rather than inward toward the family. This shift heralds the last internal task.

*Developing Personal Identity*

Developing a sense of personal identity is a very important task and incorporates elements of the other tasks. Emotionally, psychologically, and relationally adolescents begin to develop their own sense of individuality. For younger adolescents the great question is "Where do I belong?" or "Where do I fit in?" as they begin to distance themselves from their childhood influences of family and parents and begin to identify with their peers. Older adolescents begin grappling with the questions of "Who am I?" and "Who am I to become?" These are critical questions for developing adolescents and signal their move to a greater level of independence. How this move is handled by adolescents and by their parents has future implications for the relationship of parents and teens.

A helpful image for better understanding this process of individuation is to picture the family as a hand and each of the family members as fingers. Like the fingers on a hand, all family members are unique but connected to each other. During adolescence, teenagers begin to pull away from the other family members in order to develop a clearer sense of who they are as individuals. Spreading the fingers apart enables each individual finger to be seen more clearly, even though they are still all connected. Sometimes this pulling away, this process of establishing one's independence, is slow and gradual and perhaps imperceptible to the parents. And sometimes this pulling away is loud and painful and looks more like rebellion than asserting one's independence. If we don't realize that this process is both normal and necessary, we might take it personally as a sign that our children don't appreciate our efforts, or don't love us anymore. We can feel frustrated and perhaps even doubt our parenting abilities. The signs of this stage of establishing one's individuality span the range from teenagers' selection of clothing, the new color of their hair, and wanting to spend more time with their friends, to the risk behaviors of alcohol and drug use. Clearly, some expressions are more acceptable than others, but all flow from this need to set oneself apart from the very people who love them the most—parents.

Some perspective is provided by a popular saying often found on posters and cards that says: "There are only two things we can give our children that last: the first is roots and the second is wings." The roots are the experiences children have in their family and their relationship with their parents. The wings are these new expressions of individuality, of searching for one's own identity and one's place in this world. Sometimes we miss the underlying psychological task that requires that all teens spread their wings at some point, and we might be tempted to cut off our children either figuratively or literally. Remembering the image of roots and wings and trusting the relationships that we have established with our children, we can trust that these roots will keep our children connected to the family, though in a new and more mature manner. Recalling honestly how this task of separating from our own parents was handled during our adolescence is a valuable insight. And though separating from one's parents and developing one's individual identity is an adolescent issue, this task is often not accomplished during the teen years. Then the task of establishing one's own identity must be confronted later as young adults or adults...the "recovering adolescent" syndrome.

This process of separating can be a very trying and difficult time for parents. But remembering that life is a series of separations is very helpful. We need to remember back to when our children were infants and we were holding their hands so they could walk. And we knew that our child's first "official" step could only happen when the child walked without holding anyone's hand. We had to let go for our child to walk. And when we let go, our child would fall and have to get back up, and fall again and get back up again.

Then they go off to school, and we remember the first time our children got on the bus by themselves, were dropped off at school, or were walked to their classroom, and now other adults hold their hands through their times of learning. And as teens, they begin to challenge and even reject our parental guidance and values, and we have to let go again even as our children pull away and emerge into semi-adults with their own views, friends, and values.

Throughout the lives of their children, parents offer both their love and their control, but, beginning with adolescence, parents should gradually loosen their control, and that's very difficult. We need to remember that love and control have to be different with teens than with children and that, though teens outgrow their need for control, they never outgrow their need for our love.

Adolescence is a period of testing—of testing parents, school authorities, and church. Adolescence is a time of establishing one's independence. Sometimes, though, youth proclaim disbelief in old teachings—those of parents, school and church—and profess unconventional or counter-cultural opinions (anything different from what their parents hold) as a hasty declaration of freedom. Sometimes it's more for shock value than out of genuine conviction. Often they are just looking for our reaction. The wise course is to take most of what teens say and do with a grain of salt, knowing that they are searching and experimenting—unless of course their experimenting has harmful consequences, as in the case of drinking, sexual activity, and risk behaviors, when a more direct and immediate response by parents is required. This situation will be further addressed in the next chapter.

We must remember that however much our teenager comes across as self-assured, the fact is that these multiple physical and psychic explosions undermine self confidence. The adolescent feels considerable anxiety and insecurity. This is expressed in some teens by a withdrawn shyness, while others disguise this nervousness with false bravado. At age eleven children can seem so confident and secure, and by age fifteen or sixteen they can be so confused and anxious.

## THE GENERATION GAP: WHOSE CREATION?

Parenting teenagers wouldn't be nearly so difficult if we, the adults in the family, weren't also going through our own developmental changes. We don't always like to consider the fact that we never stop growing. Most all the theorists dealing with human behavior postulate a series of stages that people progress through in some sequence, whether it be in the moral, cognitive, faith, or psychological realm. Even popular conversation has become more comfortable talking about life's passages or stages. Often, though, beliefs about life's developmental stages are couched in humorous warnings about "turning thirty, forty, fifty" or "retiring at sixty-five." At whatever age, even "over the hill" minimally implies two stages of life: climbing up the hill and coasting down the other side. Adults intuitively know that they continually develop, confronting new life tasks as they do so. So what happens when the developmental growth of adult parents coincides with their teens' adolescent explosions? A generation gap is created.

Simultaneous with children entering adolescence, many parents enter middlescence, that life stage that occurs somewhere between thirty-five and forty-five years old. And the developmental tasks of each stage often conflict in four areas: identity, physical development, independence, and family and intimacy.

## THE GREAT IDENTITY QUESTION

For adolescents, the question is "Who am I?" as they begin their search for their individuality. Simultaneous for many parents of teenagers, the question is "Who am I now?" Now that the children are becoming more independent, getting themselves to school, dressing themselves, and choosing their own friends, the role of the parent must change. Even more drastic, as the last of the children graduate from high school and move out of the house, how will parents handle the "empty nest syndrome"? Or "who am I now that I am a grandparent?" The more our self-definition and identity are determined solely by our relationship with our children, the more difficult this new question: "Who am I now?" If we only know ourselves, or if our spouse and children only know us as mother or father, then when that role diminishes (though it never entirely disappears), the question "Who am I now" requires a new answer.

This great question is the impetus to the further development of identity. For adolescents, this is a time of an ever expanding self trying out new values and beliefs, determining goals, expanding one's circle of friends. For us, middlescence is often a time of consolidation in terms of career, goals, our definition of success. For the teenager the future seems boundless and open, everything seems possible, while we become painfully aware of this age of limits. We realize that we are not going to achieve everything we thought we would (back when we were teenagers). Often a move toward a more conservative lifestyle occurs. We become more conscious of retirement accounts just when our teens are so thoughtlessly spending all their own money (or our money!) on their next whim. Parents and their teenagers seem to be heading in different directions.

## PHYSICAL DEVELOPMENT

One of the built-in traps of adolescence is teens' false sense of immortality. They feel young, healthy, and strong and that they can do it all. They feel they have so much life to lead. After all, their future is far longer than their past. Many feel that nothing can hurt them. This reasoning becomes very dangerous when it serves as the basis for teens' decisions about experimenting with drugs and alcohol and sexual relationships. Some young people feel that their bodies can heal themselves, that they are strong enough or healthy enough to withstand the physical costs of using alcohol and drugs or engaging in inappropriate sexual relationships.

Experiencing the death of one of their peers is a powerful shock, whether through an accident, an illness, or as the result of suicide, because of the myth that "teenagers aren't supposed to die." Teens experience themselves physically as getting stronger and taller, and often there is little concern about caring for their physical selves. With the possible exception of young people who are involved in athletics, adolescents are the group with the least commitment to regular exercise, because their bodies don't require the same level of maintenance.

We experience something different. During middlescence we begin to confront our physical limits, and perhaps for the first time experience a fear of aging. On turning forty years old, my daughter reminded me that I was entering the "age of Bermuda shorts and black socks" and that she had noticed that I was "packing on some pounds." As a fairly dedicated runner and basketball player, this was not easy to hear from this teenager who wouldn't know regular exercise if it bit her on her couch potato. But the words ring true, even more so now that my doctor has forbidden any running because of a damaged knee. If we are finding ourselves in one-on-one competitions with our teenagers and we are not quite ready to lose gracefully, then this is a familiar reality. Physically, parents and their teenagers are heading in different directions.

And without going into too much detail, physical development is related to the physical expression of one's sexuality. At a time when a teen's sexuality is bursting, we often find ourselves rethinking our sexuality—or at least thinking more about sex. As a male I can not fully appreciate this statement by a woman friend who described menopause as "standing in the supermarket and crying over the broccoli." I suspect, though, that sex and sexuality is an issue that needs addressing in this time of middlescence for both men and women.

INDEPENDENCE

As previously described, the teenage years are characterized by a growing sense of independence. As teens struggle to appreciate and establish their own uniqueness, they pull away from the family and, therefore, from their parents. This movement often parallels the parents' growing "need to be needed." Somehow, when children are very young, their need for parents is so clear that it is not even an issue or concern. But suddenly, when we are not needed in the same way, we are more in need of some reassurance of our importance to our teenage children. We may want what our teens are unable to give, or at least unable to admit—that they need their parents. Certainly, this issue is more or less obvious to us, depending on our family and our previous relationship with our children. But acknowledging this need is a further example of how parents and their teenagers are moving in different directions.

## INTIMACY AND FAMILY

Perhaps the most common cause of tension between parents and teenagers revolves around family and family time. Just when our teenagers are moving outside their family in order to develop deeper relationships with their peers and to begin experiencing intimacy, we are often trying to recapture or reinforce a strong sense of family. When I was in elementary school my father worked several jobs, often preventing him from being home at dinner time. When I reached high school, my father changed jobs and was now home at a regular time. This occurred as I jumped into a pattern of playing sports with my neighborhood friends every day after school and into the evening hours. There was no place else I wanted to be but with the guys playing ball. My father's announcement that each dinner was to be a family meal requiring my attendance became a source of major conflicts between us.

Families will experience this tension in different ways. Our teenagers ask to vacation with their friend's family instead of going on the annual family trip. They have something else to do whenever a visit to a relative is planned. They want to have dinner with their friends. And this situation worsens when they start dating. Now they want to spend all their time with their girl or boy friend. Christmas traditions and birthday celebrations are challenged. The quickest way to start an argument is to say, "But we've always done it this way." If family celebrations and gatherings have not been the norm, trying to newly create this sense of family as our children move into adolescence will be a struggle.

For teenagers, this impetus to peer relationships is very exciting. They are experiencing intimacy outside the family, perhaps for the first time, and they feel very adult-like because they are doing the choosing in terms of friends.

This points to another source of conflict which will be addressed later—our teens' friends.

These issues lead to a natural generation gap. The simultaneous emergence of adolescence and middlescence, in both their differences and similarities, creates a tension that is normal and survivable. Recalling the previous chapter, young people need to put distance, a gap, between themselves and their parents. They have to learn how to function independently and develop their personal self-identity. Teens must forego total and comfortable dependence on their parents in order to become responsible adults. But this standing on one's own causes anxiety and fear, even as it feels exciting. We, then, have to suffer the pangs of separation and the anxiety of our children making this transition without getting hurt. We live with our doubts: "Did I do a good job of raising my kid?"

In the midst of this gap, teens are getting signals from a new and powerful source: their peer group. Because of this movement outside the family for significant relationships, the peer group challenges parents (and teachers) for the allegiance of the young. However, in this move outside the family for acceptance and affirmation, young people also feel the loss of closeness with parents and other adults who are special to them. They are pulled in two directions: the unchartered waters of independence and the safeness and security of old ties. Often, their rude, sullen, and argumentative behavior is a desperate denial of their wish to remain close.

A delicate balancing act exists for parents who support and allow the pulling away by their teens when it is safe and appropriate, while holding their arms wide open for when their children want to return to the comfort of home. If we don't understand the psychological task that underlies our children's behavior, their pulling away and wanting to be close, then we may take the pulling away as rejection and not allow for their wanting to be close. "You made your bed, now you have to lie in it" is a phrase that captures a faulty understanding of what is going on. Like the father in the parable of the prodigal son, parents must wait and watch for the "lost son" to return home. And this may be a daily routine.

Having explored these areas of concern, the issue of teens' pulling away and risk behaviors needs closer examination. We need to distinguish between symbolic rejection and real rejection. The need for teens to push against parental beliefs, values, and even rules in order to establish their own sense of individuality and independence is developmentally normal. This period of testing is more symbolic rejection when the means of testing and rejecting include clothes styles, haircuts, music, or other fads.

This testing becomes far more serious and even dangerous when the means include drinking, drug use, sexual experimentation, running away, threatening suicide, and delinquent activities. These activities are far more real rejection and are problem behaviors. We have to be able to distinguish between disturbing behaviors and disturbed behaviors. The latter activities are disturbed behaviors and require professional intervention. And just a note of caution. Since families are like a hand (to bring back a previous image), what affects one finger affects the entire hand. So one child exhibiting disturbed behaviors affects everyone and should be treated as a family issue, not just the individual child's problem. Not only will the acting-out child benefit from our support and concern, but perhaps we will uncover some unconscious way we are contributing to the problem situation. If we truly love our children, then we have to risk our culpability and become vulnerable and open to change.

Choosing to enter family counseling is a sign that the entire family, parents included, is both concerned about the situation and committed to seeking shared solutions, rather than passing blame on one person. We can contact school counselors, parish ministers, or local community social services for referrals, if counseling seems appropriate and necessary. We should contact the referred agency or counselors and ask them questions about their approach, experience with adolescents, fee structure, and availability. Counseling creates an opportunity for the entire family to address the issues causing disruption and concern, and also provides support for both the parents and their children as they struggle with new ways of behaving and relating with each other. The willingness to honestly deal with family issues through counseling really is an investment in the future of the family and a commitment to developing healthy family relationships.

## BRIDGING THE GAP

Even though this generation gap is normal and even developmentally appropriate, effective communication and good relationships with our children are still possible. In order to bridge this gap, however, both we and our teenagers must be willing to let go of some things, and also willing to build something.

The letting go is a shared task. We and our adolescents must let go of some myths if a good relationship is to be developed. These myths will be examined as they exist in both the parent and teen sphere.

| Parents | Teenagers |
|---|---|
| • "We have all the answers" | • "My parents are experts" |
| • "We have all control" | • "Convenient dependence is OK" |
| • "We are their heroes" | • "Innocence and ignorance is an excuse" |

## We Have All the Answers...
## My Parents Are Experts

First, we have to let go of "having all the answers." Wanting to be the supreme source of knowledge in every area of their teen's life is a natural parental temptation. When children are younger, appearing "all-knowing" is easier for us because children's questions and concerns are more basic. And because we start out by appearing to have all the answers, we sometimes assume that's how it will always be, or that's how it is supposed to be. This is a myth. As children move into adolescence and more into the realm of school and peers, their questions become more complex. Not only were we "never their age" because of the changing societal context in which teens now grow up and, consequently, we don't necessarily have the answers, but teens also need to struggle with finding their own answers. Even when we do know the answer, the better course might be for our teens to search out their own solutions. We can offer guidance, different perspectives or points of view, and even possible options for their dilemmas, but only when asked, and, even then, with a degree of humility, for we have now become advisors. Whether the issues concern dating, peer relationships, school concerns, employment, faith, or religion questions, we have to let go of having all the answers. And more importantly, we need to cultivate the skill of asking the right questions. For then, we can guide our teens' thinking processes, raise issues our teens may not have considered, and express our own concerns, without becoming judgmental, overbearing, or intrusive.

The following questions are appropriate for a variety of situations and are designed to enable parents to guide their teen's decision-making process. There is a decision-making model provided in the appendix of this book.

- What do you want for you? (In this situation)
- How are you feeling about this situation?
- What options or alternatives do you have?
- What are the possible consequences of these options?
- Which option seems the best to you, given what you want for you? How would it feel to choose that option?
- What do you need to do? (To get what you want for you)
- Will you do it?
- When and how will you do it?
- Will you let me know how it goes?

With practice, we can learn to add other questions, depending on the situation or issue being discussed. The underlying key is to enable our teen to identify the issue, options, and solution, and thereby create ownership for the solution and outcome.

If we have to let go of having all the answers, teens have to let go of thinking "parents are experts." Of course by the time our children enter into adolescence, many of us have already received the message from our children that we are no longer the experts. In fact, children often roll their eyes in disbelief of how little parents seem to know. Mark Twain once commented that when he was sixteen years old he couldn't believe how stupid his father was, but by the time he was twenty-one, he couldn't believe how much his old man had learned in five years. So, thinking that we are experts may be an easy myth for our teens to let go.

However, teens have to realize, especially when they are most frustrated with us, that we have received minimal training for this role of parenting. We may be well-educated, engaged in a respected profession, and very mature adults, but where did we learn how to be parents? We don't take courses and receive certificates of competence. What is the primary source of most parenting knowledge? Our parents.

Very often we find ourselves imitating our parents, using their techniques and even repeating some of their parent-like statements, despite all oaths to the contrary. But what happens if our parents were lousy parents? Many adults who are now parents themselves grew up with parents who were not always present to them, or loved them the way they needed to be loved, or related to them in supportive ways. Perhaps our parents couldn't be effective parents because they never learned how, or because their lives were too chaotic.

Or what happens when the current generation of children has needs and issues different from those of their parents and, therefore, require different parenting skills or approaches? How are these new skills and techniques developed? Usually, we practice on the first-born child! The first-born is often referred to as the experimental child because parents are trying out their parenting techniques. Adults who are the oldest child in their families all have stories of how differently they were treated than were their siblings. Or another technique for learning parenting skills is to read books like this one and watch our peers parent their children. Children have to accept that we are struggling to be the best possible parents, which means that mistakes will be made. And children must realize that our mistakes are born out of our love and concern for them. We will never be perfect, but we can be the "best possible" parents with practice and our children's patience.

### We Have All Control...
### Convenient Dependence Is OK

Second, in order to bridge the gap, parents have to "let go of their kids by lessening their control." We cannot expect to have the same control over our teenagers that we did when they were younger children. In fact, it's not healthy for teens to be treated like children because then they will never have the opportunity to develop their own life skills. Just as too little control leads to no sense of self-discipline and structure, too much control will suffocate teens. Simultaneous with our lessening control, teens have to "let go of dependence." It is very reasonable to assume that our teenagers will begin to take care of themselves, making personal decisions, and handling their personal tasks and responsibilities. Basic matters of getting themselves up for school, completing their homework, making sure they have clean clothes, and being responsible for their schedule are all examples of moving from dependency toward independence. Obviously, this move doesn't happen magically upon one's thirteenth or sixteenth birthday. Rather, personal responsibility is increased gradually throughout their grade school years, so they can develop the necessary skills for adolescence. Teens become less dependent as they learn and utilize their skills for decision making, problem solving, time and stress management, conflict management, developing friendships, and maintaining healthy relationships. The following are areas where parental control can be lessened as a teen's sense of responsibility increases.

- When to do homework
- When to do household chores
- What household chores belong to whom
- Getting oneself up for school
- How to keep one's room
- Buying one's own clothes
- Applying for a job
- Choosing a college and a major
- Choosing participation in extra-curricular activities
- Having a car, or use of the family car
- Involvement in church youth programs
- When to begin dating

- Curfews
- Determining bedtime

Using the sample questions previously provided, we can assist our children in making good decisions about these basic areas of their lives. This also teaches the skill of effective decision making which will be very important for children and teens as their decisions become more serious. When my daughter was in first and second grade, I would ask her when she came home from school whether she wanted to do her homework before dinner, which allowed TV time afterward, or after dinner, allowing for playing outside prior to dinner. The question was never "Do you want to do your homework?" It was, "When?" I controlled that she would do her homework. She controlled when, learning decision-making skills by choosing among options after considering the consequences. In high school, she had much more control over if and when she did homework, and now that she is in college, I don't have any idea how, if, or when she does homework, and I'm not sure I want to.

The previous examples describe areas where our children can begin learning basic skills, while we lessen our control and our teens lessen their dependence on us to solve all their problems and handle all their needs. The following graph illustrates the relationship between parental control and children's age—or the movement from children being dependent to independent and finally interdependent.

We should discuss together with our children where on this graph we handled the responsibility for choosing music, buying clothes, choosing our school, keeping a budget, interviewing for a job, choosing an occupation or college major, and

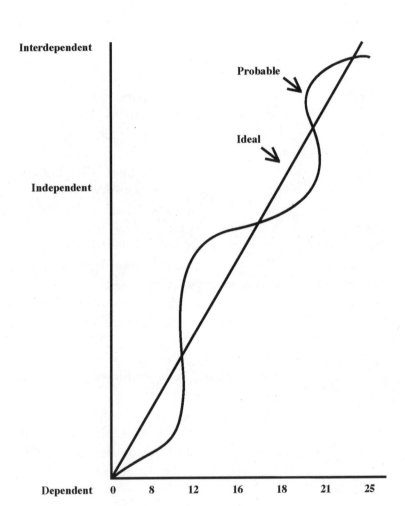

making decisions about sexual involvements. And at what age would we see our young person making these decisions?

If we foster our child's dependency too long, becoming overprotective, we run the danger of creating the eternal child. Young persons who have never had the opportunity to make any decisions that affect them, those who have all their needs met by their parents, and those who have never had to become responsible only learn dependency. They, figuratively, are not allowed to grow up, because they are kept as a child by their parents. The eternal child develops into a very immature adult and has difficulty achieving any kind of healthy independence.

The opposite, however, is also a danger. Children who are forced by their circumstances or their parents' choice to grow up too quickly are often referred to as "hurried children." These children take on adult responsibilities early in life, such as managing the household or being the primary caretakers for their siblings. Often, because they have become accustomed to adult roles, hurried children begin experimenting with other adult behaviors, such as drinking, smoking, and sexual relationships. They become independent before they have had the opportunity to develop some of the life skills necessary for adulthood, such as responsible decision making, identifying the possible consequences of one's actions, the ability to fulfill commitments, and the ability to develop healthy relationships. Sometimes, the hurried child has "done it all" by mid-adolescence and is left with little to look forward to in adulthood.

Letting go of control is a gradual process that respects our teens' growing responsibility for themselves, their personal maturity, and their self-reliance. Holding control too long can suffocate children, while letting go too soon can cause children to drown. The parental decision to loosen control must be related to the children's ability and willingness to assume personal responsibility and requires that we have the ability and an openness to negotiate with our children.

### We Are Their Heroes...
### Innocence and Ignorance Is an Excuse

The third myth needing to be let go in order to bridge the gap is "wanting to be their hero." This myth is related to the first myth of having all the answers. We just love that time of childhood when our children are younger and they think we are wonderful and perfect. We are the smartest, most talented, and all around best people children know. We are the protector, the wise sage, and the provider for the family. And being up on that pedestal does feel good, however brief the stay there. We soon go from being the most admired person in our children's life to being outdated. Our children's allegiance is transferred to the current rock musician, athlete, or movie star. The picture of us hanging in their bedroom is replaced by that of someone else. We have just to look at our children's bedroom walls in order to know their new heroes.

And while we let go of being the hero, our children must let go of their false innocence and ignorance. Though we are no longer the great protector and sage, teens make a mistake if they now look toward those other new heroes as their role models after whom they will pattern their lives. Teens have to let go of their ignorance around issues of drug and alcohol use, inappropriate sexual activity, and irresponsible driving. The "It can't happen to me"syndrome is a myth. Drug addiction, alcoholism, pregnancy, sexually transmitted diseases, and accidents do happen to teenagers. They certainly have the right to good, accurate information about these risk issues, but they also have the responsibility to consider these issues carefully. "I didn't know this could happen" reflects false innocence and ignorance.

## Communication Skills

So, bridging the generation gap requires that both parents and teenagers let go of their false myths. But just letting go of false myths alone is not enough to develop a better relationship. There has to be something put in its place. We and our teens are challenged to build a new relationship, based on effective communication, mutual respect, and trust. Communication is a common issue for all families, as evidenced by the number of books written on the subject. People are all born talkers, but genuine communication is a learned skill. Here are five practical communication skills that will enhance our relationship with our teens.

- Listen, listen, and listen
- Paraphrase
- Avoid "either/or" statements
- Use effective body language
- Use an appropriate tone of voice

The time that we spend in practicing these skills will be invaluable in fostering an open relationship with our teenagers. In the appendix of this book, Exercise #5, "Don't Say...Do Say!" is a good activity to use with our teens for identifying sentences that either hinder or help communication.

## Listen, Listen, and Listen

And listen some more. God gave people two ears and one mouth so that we'd listen twice as much as we talk. We need to listen to our children, and it's probably the most difficult when they are teenagers and when we disagree with what they are saying. We often fall into the trap of planning what we want to say while our teen is still speaking. This means we don't really hear all of what our teen is saying. Listening takes energy. We have to really focus on what our child is saying. The goal of effective listening is to truly understand what our child is saying. Understanding is not the same as agreement. We may not agree with what our children are saying, but we should work for understanding. Use Exercise # 6, "Youth–Parent Questionnaire," as a starter for conversation with your teen and as an opportunity to practice good listening skills.

## *Paraphrase*

The sign of genuine listening is the ability to repeat back not only what the child says, but also how he or she seems to feel and why. A sample formula is "You seem to feel... when you...because..." For example, "You seem a bit overwhelmed when you talk about your school work because there's so much to do." Or "You seem pretty angry when I ask you to do your chores because you don't think I'm being fair." The formula is not as important as the pieces: feeling, content, and reason. When all three pieces can be identified, genuine listening and understanding is taking place.

## *Avoid "Either/Or" Statements*

A common parental approach to an argument may sound something like "Either you do what I say, or you're grounded forever". And the natural inclination is for teenagers to see how long we can stand them around the house. We should never say "either you... or..." unless we are ready and able to carry out the "or." These statements really box us into a corner, giving us only the option of carrying through on the consequence or losing respect. A more effective approach is to give our children options and thereby enable them to develop their decision-making skills. So, instead of "Either you cut the grass today or you're in for the weekend," a better phrasing might be "On which day would you rather cut the grass?"—which is not to say, "Do you want to cut the grass?" Giving teens options and choices within some parameters gives them control over the use of their time, and teaches them about decisions and consequences.

## Use Effective Body Language

When talking with teens, don't be doing something else that's distracting, like reading the paper. We demonstrate that we are giving full attention to our teenager by maintaining good eye contact, facing our teen, and leaning forward if either is sitting down. Non-verbal support and encouragement by giving a smile, a hug, a wink, a pat on the shoulder, nodding the head, or reaching for our child's hand is very important. Body language is even more effective than the words used when communicating, so we should pay attention to what our body language—and, conversely, what our child's body language—is communicating.

## Use An Appropriate Tone of Voice

The tone of voice is very important in effective communication. Our tone should not come across to our children as sarcastic, all-knowing, or even disinterested when responding to our children or when our children are sharing something with us. Our use of encouraging phrases with a genuine tone of voice demonstrates our interest and keeps the conversation going. Phrases that are helpful include

"And then what happened? What did you do next? How did that feel? Tell me more about that."

This chapter has described the internal developmental tasks of young people, the natural generation gap between parents and teens that is created, and ways of bridging this gap in parent–teen relationships. Additional strategies will be described in the following chapters and various exercises and activities are provided in the appendix.

# 3 · Practical Parenting...Giving Youth Roots and Wings

Balancing our teens' need for connection to the family and independence from the family will never be easy. As we struggle to provide both roots and wings, we should remember that there is no "one right way" to parent. Our parenting styles are influenced by our parents, family customs, ethnic heritage, family configuration and makeup, and even by the neighborhood in which we live. These strategies and guidelines, therefore, should be adapted, molded, and refined to fit your family situation and your needs.

You may want to consider using Exercise # 2 in the appendix, "Survey on Parent–Teen Relationships," as a way of taking a "temperature check" on the current state of your relationship. The following guidelines might make more sense after an initial discussion with your teen.

STRATEGIES AND GUIDELINES

The following tips are not meant to be an all-encompassing list that will guarantee happy relationships with our children and teenagers. This list has been developed through conversations with parents and with teenagers and provides some guidelines for setting family rules, handling consequences, and developing relationships.

## RECOGNIZE TEENS' NEED FOR STABLE RULES

Everyone needs to know the rules, whether it be in the home, at work, in school, or in society. Teens benefit from stable rules. During adolescence when they begin to experiment with their own individuality, they need something to rebel against. Pushing against parental rules is natural. In the exercise approach called isometrics, a person pushes various muscles against an immovable object in order to develop that muscle group. Family rules provide the object against which adolescents push, in order to develop their inner emotional, psychological, and personal muscles—their sense of right and wrong, appropriate and inappropriate behavior, following directions and learning obedience. But if every time they push, the rules collapse, then they don't learn anything. They don't develop any inner strengths.

So our rules must be stable, but that doesn't mean they have to be rigid and unchangeable. For example, even though a teen's curfew is usually 10:00 p.m., on the night of a special school dance the rule might be changed to a later time. Now, that doesn't mean that the rule has to be changed for any or every reason—every request isn't a "special" event. However, rules should be flexible depending on circumstances, and revised at times to honor a teen's growing independence and maturity. Families certainly shouldn't have the same rules for a sixteen year old that they had for a six year old.

## HAVE CLEAR EXPECTATIONS

We need to share our expectations concerning our children's behavior in our home, at school, when visiting relatives, and when they are with their friends. In developing or changing the rules, our expectations should be clearly articulated. Teens are skilled at finding the loopholes, so we have to be clear about both the "letter and spirit" of their expectations. Does curfew mean to be in the home or just on the property? Who is included in not having anyone in the house while the parents are out? Does bedtime mean lights out and TV off?

Involving children in developing family expectations is very valuable. When children have some input, they are more likely to "own" the rules. This involvement is also an opportunity to teach children how to negotiate, compromise, and discuss reasons for rules. Identifying certain benchmarks when expectations can be reviewed and changed is also very important. For instance, on birthdays, school graduations, or other important dates, parents and children might sit down and review the rules and negotiate changes. Curfews, for instance, might be reviewed on one's birthday, or at the beginning of summer. Knowing that the rules change as they get older makes it easier for children to accept and follow the current rules, even when they don't like them.

## HAVE LOGICAL CONSEQUENCES

Along with stable rules and clear expectations, we need logical consequences when the rules and expectations are not met. Logical consequences are fair and fit the problem. They are not excessive nor too lenient. For instance, when teens come home after curfew, they might lose an equivalent amount of time on their next night out. Grounding them for a week when they are an hour late might be excessive and seem like an overreaction. Ignoring the curfew violation is perhaps too lenient, suggesting that the curfew isn't really important.

Involving children in determining the consequences is a very good technique. This assists teens in identifying logical consequences. When teens make a decision leading to negative consequences, let the consequences speak for themself and let the child live with them. For instance, if teens choose to come home late, then they live with the consequences. It's really fair to say, "You made this decision and this is the consequence of your decision." That is better than saying, "You came in late and now I have to punish you," or "Here's your punishment." To be harsh or authoritarian just fuels further conflict. No parent wants to be in the role of judge, jury, and jailer. If we have clear expectations and logical consequences, then our children have the freedom of making decisions and accepting the consequences. Children can choose to not study or not do homework, and live with the consequences of failed tests or poor grades. They can choose to spend their allowance on something they want, and live with the consequence of not having money for something else. They make decisions and live with the consequences, and we avoid having an emotional fight.

The limit to teens' freedom to make decisions and live with the consequences is when their decision may lead to physical, emotional, or spiritual harm. For instance, we can't stand by and let our teens make the decision to drink and drive, and then let them live with the consequences, which may include harm to the teen and/or to others. Several of these important issues will be further discussed in exercise 4 in the appendix.

## DECIDE WHICH ISSUES ARE IMPORTANT

We don't have to win every fight or battle with our children. When we are willing to give in on an issue, we teach our children how to "win," by saying "You're right about this," and we model how to "lose" or compromise, by saying "I'm sorry." Every issue isn't life or death. So we have to decide which can be used as learning experiences, and which we have to win for the benefit of our children. Parents should first discuss these issues together so that there's a united front when dealing with their children. Then they should discuss these issues with their teens. Exercise # 4, "Parent–Teen Conflict Resolution" provides rules for "fighting fair." A side benefit of working through these issues with your teens is teaching them conflict resolution, which is a very important life skill. Some issues where we can let go include:

### *Clothes*

This is an area where our children should have choices and be able to make decisions. We will never understand "what's in and what's out" with youth today. And clothes are very important during this period of searching for acceptance from their peers. This doesn't mean, however, that we should have to buy our children whatever they want and whenever they want it. We can make buying clothes an opportunity for teaching our children some basic life skills by giving them a budget for clothing and letting them spend it however they want. They make decisions, consider options, and live with the consequences. And we save our blood pressure.

## *Their Rooms*

We always have the option of closing the door to our children's room! Controlling the cleanliness of their rooms is an opportunity for children to live with the consequences of disorderly rooms, piles of dirty clothes, and lost possessions. One technique that is usually effective for getting children to clean their rooms is to encourage them to invite friends for an overnight. Even if this technique doesn't work, the cleanliness of their room is not a reflection on us, and gives some room for negotiation for the rest of the house: "You can choose to keep your room how you want it, but since we all live in the rest of the house, we have to find an acceptable compromise."

## *Music*

Music has always been an avenue for teens' rebellion. Witness the reaction by previous generations of parents to Elvis Presley, the Beatles, or our favorite singers when we were teenagers. Certainly, some music today expresses negative values and uses harsh language. But much music also expresses positive values, even if the music is loud and the words seem incomprehensible. Besides, forbidding teens to buy certain types of music is an almost impossible task. They will just listen to the banned albums somewhere else and we won't be around to talk about the values expressed in the lyrics. Rather, when dealing with controversial music, we should listen to the songs with our children and read the words together. Then together discuss the values in the song. Ask, "Is this what you believe about relationships? About love? About sex? About life? Why do you believe this?" At least we are part of the more important discussion. We can also negotiate limits on the sound volume, so we don't have to listen to the music.

Another important point to remember: Never attack the artist or the group or the type of music, e.g. rap, heavy metal, alternative, etc. All music has pluses and minuses. We show our children that we are being fair by avoiding generalizations and stereotyping. Keep the discussion on the values expressed in the music: "I'm against the values in this song." That way, the discussion centers on values, rather than on how a music group looks and acts. This approach takes some work, but it's worth it—and we can teach our children critical thinking skills. Besides, we don't have to pay for our children's music. Let them pay for their music with their own money. Again, this fosters decision-making skills, considering options, and living with consequences.

## Their Friends

One of the most difficult and sensitive issues between parents and teenagers is their friends. Youth react strongly to parental criticism about their friends because of the importance of their peer group, an issue described previously. Rather than criticize, we should make an effort to know our children's friends. We should invite them into our home, have snacks and refreshments—a very important sign of hospitality—and talk to them. Spending time enables us to really know our children's friends, while their friends get to know us and our expectations and values. Teens really appreciate their parents' accepting their friends without criticism. Furthermore, since identification with the peer group is so strong, by accepting our children's friends we are publicly accepting our children. Besides, we can learn much about our teens' interests and values by the values and interests of the friends they choose. So we should work to make our home "teen-friendly."

So far, we have looked at several issues where we can bend, compromise, and even give in to our children. However, there are several interrelated issues which are important for us to win because of the potential consequences to our children: parties, drinking, driving, and sexual activity.

## Parties

Beginning with our children's first invitation to a party or another child's home, we should ask basic questions: Will the parents be home? What's the phone number? How long is the party? When our children are younger we probably drive them to their parties, giving us the opportunity to introduce ourselves to the host, clarify pick-up times, and also check out the party. As our children get older, we do less transporting, but our concerns should increase. Will there be parents present? Will they be in the room where the party is being held? Will there be alcohol? We are being very fair in asking our teens these questions and also to contact the party host. Occasionally, the media carry stories about parents allowing drinking at their homes, rationalizing that teens are going to drink anyway and that it's better to drink and stay overnight rather than having the teens drive home after drinking. We should be clear that it is unacceptable for other adults to make choices about alcohol and our children. We need to be vigilant about the party issue.

## Drinking

We have to discuss this issue with children. We must express our expectations and our reasons. Alcohol is a depressant that inhibits one's ability to make good decisions. Drinking is often an activity that symbolizes moving out of childhood and into young adulthood. We should probably remove the mystery surrounding alcohol, emphasizing that responsible behavior, not drinking itself, is the issue. If alcoholism runs in the family, young people need to know this and the potential physical consequences. Alcohol relates to the following issues.

## Driving

Receiving one's driving license is a very important benchmark of entering young adulthood, and therefore this is a very powerful control. We should be very clear about our expectations concerning driving. Unsafe driving practices by teenagers must carry clear consequences—for instance, paying for their own tickets, insurance costs, or repairs. If teens miss curfew because they were driving friends home, then perhaps they lose use of the car for a night. Parents might want to declare drinking and driving a non-negotiable issue. "If I ever smell alcohol in the car, you will lose your license." These issues need discussion, clear expectations, and logical consequences.

## Sexual Activity

Sexuality is a difficult topic for many parents and teens to discuss. Yet adolescence is marked by an exploding sexual awareness, bombardment by media sexual images, and teens' searching for intimacy. We have to begin talking with our children about physical development, sexuality, and sexual decision making at appropriate ages. We are being unrealistic if we think that having "the talk" with our children in elementary school or when our teen reaches high school is enough to assist our teen in dealing with the conflicting messages, feelings, and decisions that surround sexuality. Teens need an opportunity to ask their questions and learn accurate information, especially from their parents. For many teens who become sexually active, alcohol often plays a role in their decision making—or their inability to make a responsible decision. All of this points to a need for clear communication between parents and their teens.

Inevitably, there will be other issues confronting parents and their teens. We need to balance where we can afford to let go of control and where we can't.

## BE VIGILANT, BUT RESPECT YOUR TEEN'S PRIVACY

Young people have a right to their personal privacy. They have a need for physical privacy in terms of a space to call their own. This is a real challenge in families where bedrooms are shared. And teens have a need for personal space where they can be alone at times. During adolescence some teens begin spending more time alone. They seem more withdrawn, even sullen. They are carving out some space for themselves. Some teens find their privacy in keeping diaries. Even with the best of intentions, reading a child's diary is a major intrusion. This breach of trust is very difficult to mend.

Another way teens establish their space is by controlling how much information they share with their parents. Perhaps you have had your questions answered with one syllable words or grunts. A common parent–teen conversation might sound like this: "Where are you going?" "Out." "What are you going to do?" "Hang out." "When will you be back?" "Later." They are not necessarily being difficult intentionally. By controlling their responses to our questions, they are experiencing a sense of personal power and space. They are simply struggling to create some personal boundaries in order to better understand who they are. In order to survive peacefully, families may have to negotiate answering with more than four words. Of course that means we can't hide behind, "Because I said so," as a reason for teens to do what they have been told.

Traditionally, teens have also used language to create a sense of secrecy and privacy by speaking in their own terms and words. We should not be hesitant to ask what their terms mean. For example, "going with" as a description for relationships has had different connotations over the past generations. Each generation has had its own terms for various levels of relationships, various groups or types of youth (sports, brains, grunges, nerds, preps, etc.), and for various activities ("let's party" has had various meanings). We don't need to know the exact definition of everything our teenagers say or mean, but when necessary, we should ask for a clarification or meaning and not assume we know what our children are talking about.

In addition to carving out their individual space through their conversations with their parents, sometimes children will become less open and willing to share about school, their friends, or their activities. Withdrawing from conversation or withholding information and becoming more secretive may also be a way for teens to establish their identity. Information is power, and controlling how much we know about them, their friends, and their activities is a way for teens to experience personal power. However, a sudden turn to total secrecy may be a sign that a teen is engaging in behavior that might upset us.

Even though privacy is important, we should still be aware of what our teens are doing, with whom they are associating, and where they are spending time or "hanging out." Through genuinely interested questions, time spent together, having their friends in our house, attending parent–teacher meetings at school, and involvement in their other activities where appropriate, we can have a good sense of what is happening in the lives of our children.

## RESPECT THEIR INDIVIDUALITY

This struggle to carve out a space for themselves is a reminder to us to be especially attentive to teens as individuals. Teens need to feel accepted as themselves. They need to be appreciated as unique persons who are developing their own sense of values, beliefs, goals, and interests. Even when the changes aren't necessarily noticeable, we have to remember the internal explosions that are happening. The changes are there and it's both wonderful and frightening. The changes are wonderful in that the child is becoming his or her own person, taking more responsibility for his or her life. And that's also frightening. The teen is now caught between the security and comfort of home and family and the fascination of the peer group and the rest of their world.

We need to respect our teens as individuals, with their new experiences, concerns, dreams, and desires. We have to remember that, despite the fact that adolescence has been happening for quite a while, this is the first time for this child. And our teen will experiment with different persona, as expressed in their clothes, music, activities, language, and friends. During this time, teens may become someone that we don't like, someone who is different from the person we expected them to become. We have to be careful of the conscious and unconscious expectations that we have for our children, because this is a time when teens may disappoint us, especially when they appear to be someone other than our ideal image of what teens should be. This time of growth and experimentation is important in order for teens to develop their sense of individuality. Perhaps we need to hang up the poster with the saying, "Be patient. God isn't finished with me yet." This poster may have been designed for teenagers, for they really are works in progress. Some solace and comfort can be drawn from the adage, "The fruit doesn't fall far from the tree." In the long term, children will pick up most of their parents' values, though lived out in their unique manner.

In families with more than one child moving through adolescence, it is especially important for parents to pay attention to each of their children specifically. Traditions such as taking the child out to breakfast or dinner on their birthday, or allowing children to choose their own birthday dinner at home, or occasional outings just with the individual child are ways of acknowledging their special importance. Children are simultaneously members of the family and individuals and they need to be treated as both. Indeed, guarding teens' individuality while fostering their sense of belonging is a balancing act for parents, but one filled with rewards.

## WASTE TIME WITH YOUR TEENS

In the desire to develop a meaningful and loving relationship with their children while fulfilling all their commitments and responsibilities as adults, many parents try to carve out opportunities for "quality time" with their children. At times, this desperate attempt leads to an overabundance of organized activities. We are tempted to equate our success as parents with the number of clubs, sports, and activities in which our children participate. We might fall into the "chauffeur" style of parenting, living by a calendar of commitments and driving responsibilities. Sometimes parents, and their children, forget for whose benefit all of this activity is planned. This lifestyle may also blind us to a basic value: it's the time we waste on our children that makes our children feel important.

Wasting time is especially challenging, and seems almost sinful, in a society that values time for what can be accomplished or produced within its confines. But genuine conversation happens best during the less stressed, less structured, and more free time. Without the pressure of an agenda or schedule, more serious questions and concerns arise. During these times, bonds of trust and genuine communication are created. Sharing opinions about school, community, church, national, and global issues and listening to our children's views is a very important expression of respect. We are signaling that our teens have opinions that are worth listening to, especially if we don't necessarily agree with those opinions. Consider using some of the questions in exercise # 9, "Dinner Table Discussion," as conversation starters. But remember, teens will often take a view that is contrary to their parents' view just as a means of establishing a sense of independence. So relax, listen, ask for their opinions and waste time, for the benefit of the entire family.

## LOVE YOUR TEENS UNCONDITIONALLY

Sometimes young people get the message that love is earned, that being loved is based on getting good grades, making the sports team, going to the right school, or having the right friends. Being loved is tied into feeling accepted, and feeling accepted is integral to one's self-esteem. But this is conditional love. Conditional love is probably the greatest source of stress for children, for they find themselves constantly trying to live up to artificial criteria in order to be loved.

Unconditional love is a free gift. Persons are loved because of who they are, not because of what they do, what they own, or what they accomplish. Children need unconditional love from their parents. We need to tell our children, and especially when they become teenagers, that we love them. Don't assume they know they are loved. During the explosions of adolescence very little, if anything, is certain for teenagers. They need to hear they are loved, loved for who they are. We need to love our children the way we did when we had more control over them. Children never outgrow their need for love, though they do outgrow their need for control.

We also have to remember that our children love us, even if they have difficulty expressing this love. Believing in unexpressed love is perhaps the most difficult when children or teens make a decision that has painful consequences. What is the most appropriate reaction if our teen becomes pregnant, or is arrested, or engages in some other negative behavior? Unconditional love says "I may not like or agree with your decision, but you are more important than what you did." This does not imply that consequences are avoided or downplayed. However, the parental task is to love our children unconditionally and intentionally.

Exercise #3 in the appendix, "The ABCs of Showing Love," is effective for identifying many different ways we and our teens can show love to each other.

## TELL YOUR CHILDREN THAT
## THEY ARE DOING A GOOD JOB

Affirmation is very important. Sometimes teenagers just need to hear that they are doing OK. In their struggle to establish their own identity, to be part of the family even as they pull away, and to negotiate the ups and downs of adolescence, it is very easy for teens to be highly self-critical. They find it easier to name their faults than their strengths and to identify their shortcomings rather than their accomplishments. We should, for no special reason, just let our teens know that they are doing a fine job of growing up. A popular adage states that in order to make it in life, everyone needs just one person who is absolutely sold on him or her. We should be that person for our children. Tell them, "I am absolutely sold on you," "You are doing a good job of growing up," "You have become a wonderful teenager," "I am proud of you." Of course, this does not prevent the next round of conflicts, issues, and confrontations. But affirmation does create an atmosphere where the tensions can be handled and love is not forgotten.

It is a challenge to balance affirmation or the positive reinforcement of our children and the inevitable criticism of teens' inappropriate behavior. A good rule of thumb is to provide four affirmations or positive strokes for every critique or negative comment. If we really want our children to listen to a critique of their behavior, then critique must be balanced with affirmations, though not at the same time. There is no faster way to undo a positive affirmation than by adding the conjunction "but." "This is an excellent report card, but what about this math grade?" "Your room looks really clean, but your clothes are still in a pile." "Thank you for completing your chores, but you didn't tie up the trash bags." By separating our affirmation from our critique, both can be heard more clearly.

This balance of affirmation and critique is true especially for teenagers because their self-esteem takes such a beating anyway during the explosions of adolescence. Teens often believe that they only hear from adults when they have made a mistake or that the only time parents pay any attention to them is when they have done something wrong. As one teen said to me during a phone call in which she painfully shared her desire to commit suicide, "I hate my parents. They never say anything when I do well in school or if I do my chores. But just let me mess up once and they are in my face. They only pay attention to me when I do something wrong. But sometimes negative attention is better than no attention at all." As described in chapter 1, children of all ages hunger for recognition and the affirmation that they are OK.

Finding four (at least) opportunities to compliment teens can be challenging. But if we want to avoid becoming solely the bearer of bad news and if we want our children to take our critique seriously, then we have to also affirm the behaviors, the decisions, and even the attitudes that are positive. In fact, by complimenting our children, we are actually affirming the behavior we want them to exhibit. For instance, when we say, "I appreciate the way you helped clear the dinner table (or did your homework, finished your chores, talked with your grandparents, etc.)," we are identifying the behaviors we value. Positive affirmations reinforce behavior, because everyone likes compliments. So look for opportunities to honestly praise the specific behaviors and actions that you desire in your children. Remember: "You are doing a good job of growing up. You are becoming so mature and self-reliant. I am really proud of you." A practical skill for effectively affirming children will be more fully described in the next chapter.

## THE GREATER BURDEN IS ON THE ADULT

Given the natural generation gap that developmentally exists between parents and their adolescent children, the greater burden of responsibility to bridge this gap is on the adults. After all, we have more experience, more maturity, and more insight, if not more patience. This doesn't lessen the responsibility of teens to work at bridging the gap, but it's not a 50/50 proposition. Exercise #1, "10 Ways to Get Along With Parents," could be discussed with your teens, and followed with exercise #7, "I Think We'd Get Along Better If..." as a way of identifying possible steps toward improved relationships.

We have to be willing to take the first step. That may mean offering reconciliation, or saying "I'm sorry," "Can we talk?" "I miss talking to you," or "I miss sharing with you." By modeling forgiveness, genuine listening, and effective communication we model what it means to be in relationship.

Our own adolescent years serve as a reminder that teenagers change, parents change, and their relationship will change. In families where there is much verbal, emotional, and perhaps even physical pain, some parents feel rejected or that they have failed, and they are tempted to burn their bridges and end their relationship with their teens. These parents, especially, have to keep perspective and take the long view about their relationships with their children.

Adolescence is a time of testing and pushing against parental and other limits. It is a time of questioning and challenging. The challenge is to keep perspective, be patient, and remember that children who navigate adolescence with their parents' support and love become the young adults who support and love their parents.

# 4 · Self-Esteem and Life Skills: Making Champions of our Children

Self-esteem is a concept that is receiving much attention in education, family, and societal arenas today. Everyone seems concerned about how children and youth feel about themselves, recognizing the impact that self-esteem has on how one perceives his or her own value, abilities, and sense of the future. However, self-esteem is not an easy concept to define. For the purposes of this chapter, self-esteem is understood as a belief in oneself, a sense of self-worth and self-respect that comes from thoughts, feelings, sensations, and experiences. Self-esteem reflects the extent to which our teenagers believe they are capable, significant, and successful.

A child's self-esteem is influenced by many factors: parents and family, school environment, peer group, church involvement, community involvement, and other significant adults. Self-esteem is reflected in one's values, educational aspirations, positive view of the future, ability to make friends, ability to make good decisions, school performance, and willingness to try new experiences, as well as in one's faith life.

LOVEABLE AND CAPABLE

Perhaps the most succinct definition of self-esteem lies in the title of a short, elaborately-illustrated parable from my youth, "I Am Loveable and Capable." In the story a boy, whose name I have long forgotten, gets up in the morning and puts on his IALAC sign (I am loveable and capable). The story follows the boy through his day at school, filled with a variety of positive and negative experiences affecting his IALAC sign. With each of those experiences which lessen his self-esteem, such as losing his homework, having a car splash mud on his clothes, getting hassled by a group of older bullies, and being yelled at by his parents for coming home late, a piece of his IALAC sign is torn off. For each positive experience, such as a teacher's compliment, correctly answering a question in school, and having a girl classmate say hello, a piece of his sign is added on. On this particular day, the negatives outweigh the positives, so that when he finally goes to bed, his IALAC sign is the size of a postage stamp.

Every child wears an IALAC sign. Some signs are more resilient than others, some are more durable, and some are steadily disappearing. The IALAC sign is a useful image to describe the impact that parents and all who interact with children and youth have on their self-esteem.

Two very important components are included in the IALAC concept: loveable and capable. Children and youth need to know they are loveable because of who they are, without requirements. In the previous chapter, unconditional acceptance and love require that we place no conditions on our love for our children and teenagers. Unconditional love doesn't mean that we always love what our children do, but unconditional love does challenge us to separate our reaction to the behavior from our feelings for the person. Parents may not like the action or behavior, e.g. breaking curfew, failing a school subject, or even drinking or trying drugs, but parents need to be clear that their love is not based on what their children do, but on who their children are as their sons and daughters.

Unconditional love also says love is not based on the good things our children do. For example, parents shouldn't give their children the message that they love them because they get good grades, make the sports team, or do their chores. The trap in giving this message is that if their children fail a course, get cut from a team, or forget their chores, they may think that their parents no longer love them. Children may see parental love as based on their accomplishments, and that's very conditional.

With their peers this conditional acceptance is even more serious. Often, teenagers think their acceptance by their peers is based on what they own, how they dress, whom they date, or where they live; such is very conditional acceptance. But given the power of the peer group when young people begin to pull away from their parents and family, this conditional acceptance is very powerful nonetheless.

So a very important task for all parents is convincing their children that they are loveable. And, as discussed in the previous chapter, to love them means to set boundaries and limits. Rarely, however, do our children understand that setting limits and rules is a reflection of our parental love. So even as we strive to love our children for who they are, our children may seem not to like us in return. However, at this stage of development, for parents, being respected may be more important than being loved. So good parents love their children, they tell their children that they love them, and they act in a way that shows their love, hoping in some way to convince their children that they are loveable.

But...young people need more than our affirmation and love. Because adolescents are in this stage of physical and emotional change, conflicting values, and relational explosions, affirmation has to be connected to adolescents' experience of themselves, if the affirmation is to be seen as authentic. Our teens may unconsciously believe that we have to love them because we are their parents and it's in our job description. Parental affirmation may seem meaningless and empty if a child does not believe or accept that affirmation, if a child feels unloveable. For affirmation and love to be experienced as authentic by children and teenagers, this affirmation has to be connected to the second characteristic of IALAC—capable. Affirmation seems more genuine when the words of affirmation are connected to youths' experience of themselves as able to do things.


LIFE SKILLS

This understanding of "capable" is different from success at sports and school. "Capable" in terms of self-esteem is rooted in competence and confidence, in children's ability to handle basic life situations and issues. Capable means having mastery of the basic life skills that are needed to simply survive and interact in a complex society. Life skills include a person's ability to form various types of relationships, to develop plans of action, and to handle the natural stress and anxiety caused by life. Examples of life skills include the ability to make friends, handle a job, follow directions, set goals, solve problems, respond to others' needs, accept and offer forgiveness, manage one's time, listen to others, express oneself, communicate with others, resolve conflicts, be sensitive to others, handle social situations, manage stress, and so on. Perhaps we have taken these skills for granted, because after all, as we were growing up, learning these skills probably just happened. We probably weren't even aware of learning these skills. Yet, today, many young people have not learned these basic life skills, and that negatively impacts their self-esteem. Exercise #10, "Making Good Decisions: The DECIDE Approach," provides a clear outline that you and your teen could use together when dealing with a decision. In so doing, you will be helping your teen learn the life skill.

In the past, learning these skills was less complex because guidelines for behavior were more clear and constantly supported by group norms, i.e. the neighborhood, school, and church. But in a changing society, and given the impact of television and other media, young people today are confronted with a variety of value systems, belief systems, behaviors, and environments, and often without regard for fostering positive behaviors. Watching how television handles conflict resolution where the biggest gun always seems to win, and how it depicts relationships and commitment where "touch and go" relationships seem to be the norm, are examples of how important life skills are not reinforced in the medium that impacts young people.

There is a need to affirm children's and teens' capabilities specifically, identifying the behavior that we like and the reasons we like it. This ability to identify and affirm good behaviors is a very important parenting skill. We have only two ways to change children's behaviors: to reinforce the good and correct the bad. When we manage children's behavior by reinforcing the good, we are acknowledging a skill or competence and that makes the behavior or life skill repeatable.

For instance: when parents tell their child, "You did a very nice job of cleaning up your room. Your clothes are put away, your school books are piled neatly, and your bed is made. I am pleased because now your room will look nice for company," not only have they affirmed their child's skill in cleaning the room, but they have also identified the elements of that skill, and they have given a reason for using

that skill. The skill of cleaning one's room includes the elements of putting clothes away, stacking books, and making
the bed. The parents have taught the skill of cleaning the
room, reinforced the behavior, and affirmed the child's
sense of feeling capable. And the parents have given their
child a reason for using this skill, other than "I said so!"

Another example with a teenager: "Thanks very much
for calling us and telling us you were going to be late. We
really worry about you when you are late, so we appreciated
knowing where you were and when you'd be home." Teen
responsibility includes informing parents when they will be
late, and these parents have identified the reasons why they
want to know about late arrivals home. This is much more
effective than, "Just wait until you get home! If you can't
handle the curfew then you are grounded!" However, that
doesn't mean that there aren't times when there have to be
consequences for behaviors, which will be described later.

So, in terms of self-esteem, young people need to feel
loveable and capable. Children and youth need to be
accepted for who they are, and they need to have their basic
life competencies identified and affirmed. When we identify our children's skills and gifts, we contribute to their
experience of uniqueness and specialness. When young
people are able to use their life skills in situations which
require those skills, their sense of personal self-confidence
is fostered. Feeling capable enhances their self-esteem.

You will notice in the above examples that life skills are all
identifiable behaviors. A life skill is observable. Exercise # 8,
"Trustworthiness," uses six identifiable behaviors to measure
the level of trust and trustworthiness in your parent–teen
relationship. Although we all have three capabilities—thinking, feeling, and behavior—only behavior can be seen. When
a person changes the way he or she is thinking or feeling,
that's an internal change and may not be observable to anyone else. We really don't know what a person is thinking or

feeling—unless it is expressed in behavior. A change in behavior is an external change, and it's measurable, observable, and identifiable. Because children's and teens' sense of being capable is rooted in their behavior, we want to teach behaviors that will enable them to feel confident and competent in life situations. We are much more likely to act our way into a new way of thinking than we are to think our way into a new way of acting. By teaching new ways of acting, new life skills, we will be affecting our children's way of thinking and believing about themselves.

For example, when a child says, "Why do I have to go to Mass on Sunday?" this is a teaching discussion, not a theological discussion. "You are going because someday you will need faith." Later, we can talk with him or her about God, faith, and prayer, but for right now, going to Mass is the behavior, the life skill, that we want. "Why do I have to go to grandmom's house?" "Because spending time with family is important to us." Family involvement is the behavior, the life skill, that we want.

## PRACTICAL STRATEGIES FOR DEVELOPING LIFE SKILLS

Father Flanagan's Boys' Home in Boys' Town, Nebraska has done much research into strategies that are effective in fostering life skills in children and young people. Three such strategies have been identified which we can use to reinforce positive behaviors and also teach new life skills. These strategies do not replace parenting; rather they are incorporated into our current parenting style. Good parents probably already use these or similar approaches unconsciously, but a careful description of these three strategies—effective praise, preventive teaching, and corrective teaching—can be very beneficial.

*Effective Praise*

This technique encourages and reinforces positive behavior by identifying the elements of a positive behavior or life skill. Listen to the difference between these two praise statements.

> "Shannon, thank you for paying attention to me while I've been talking to you." And...

> "Shannon, thank you for paying attention to me while I've been talking to you. You have looked me in the eyes, nodded your head, and even smiled once when I was talking. It shows me that you have been listening and I appreciate that."

Obviously, the second praise statement not only affirms the behavior, but identifies the elements of the behavior. If a child doesn't really know what "paying attention" means, then this praise statement reinforces the behavior, while teaching the skill. This example is similar to the "child cleaning his/her room" and the "teen calling because he/she is going to be late for curfew" examples used above. Praise is more effective when we can identify the elements of the skill or behavior, and the reason this skill is good to have. Effective praise includes three components:

- Show approval of the behavior
- Identify the elements of the behavior
- Give a reason why the behavior is important

Imagine what effective praise would sound like in the following situations:

• Your teen finishes a school project on time (or early!). ("Nice job in completing your school project. You really planned well, stuck to your priorities, and managed your time. That's a real sign of taking responsibility.")

- Your teen decides not to go to a party which had you worried.

("I think you made a very good decision and I know it wasn't easy for you. But you weighed all the possible consequences and chose what was best for you. That takes a degree of real maturity.")

- Your teen gets up for school on his/her own.

("Nice job of getting up on your own. You picked the right time for you, set the clock, and got everything done in time for school. You really are taking more control over your life and you make mornings easier on me.")

Chapter 3 stressed the importance of a 4 to 1 ratio of affirming our children to critiques. Utilizing the skill of "effective praise" enables us to do so.

A subtle use of effective praise concerns the third step in the technique: giving a reason why the behavior is important. When possible, we should give reasons for the behavior that impacts other people. For instance, when children listen, not only will they hear what's being said, but they also make the speaker feel good. When a teen makes a good decision, not only is the teen acting more responsible, but the parents feel better about how their child is maturing. When our children are quiet at the movie theater, not only can they hear the movie, but the rest of the audience can hear also. We can begin at their very early ages teaching our children to act in particular ways because of how their behavior affects other people. By teaching "other-centered" rationales for doing the behavior, we are introducing our children to moral behavior and moral thinking.

*Preventive Teaching*

This skill identifies a necessary behavior or skill by describing the elements of the skill and the reason the skill or behavior is desired. This technique teaches the necessary skill prior to the skill actually being needed. Doing so fosters a sense of confidence in a child or teen because the youngster will know how to act in a particular situation. For example:

> "Shannon, when your grandparents are visiting, could you please be polite and sociable, by entering into conversation, listening to them while they are speaking, and staying at the dinner table until dinner is completely finished? That way your grandparents will know that you care about them. Does that make sense to you? Can I see that 'I'm interested' look you have? Thanks, I really appreciate your willingness to hang out with your grandparents."

Preventive teaching includes five components:

- Describe the behavior that is desired.
- Give a reason why the behavior is important.
- Have them acknowledge what you are saying.
- Practice the behavior, if appropriate.
- Praise and affirm them.

Imagine what preventive teaching would sound like in the following situations:

- Preparing your teen for driving with other teens.
("Andy, soon you will be driving with your friends in the car. Can we agree on some basic ground rules, such as you will always drive safely and there will never be anyone who has been drinking in the car? If someone has been drinking, even if they are a close friend of yours, they may do something that interferes with your driving and possibly cause an accident. And if someone was ever injured while you were

driving, I think you'd feel terrible. Does that make sense? If you're not sure how to avoid a situation, I'd rather you call me and we will figure out a plan. OK? Thanks, Andy. I feel confident about your driving.")

• Preparing your teen for going out to parties where drinking might occur.

("Regina, now that you are starting to go to parties, I think we need to discuss handling parties where alcohol might be present. I hope you will have the strength to resist the temptation by saying something like, 'No thanks, I don't like beer.' Or 'No thanks, I'm still drinking this coke.' Have you thought about how you'll handle someone offering you something to drink? What would you say? Can we practice your 'favorite line'? And you can always call me if things are getting out of control. I just have a real fear about parties and alcohol. Does my concern make sense? Thanks, Regina. I feel good about your handling tough situations.")

• Preparing your teen for handling dating situations which could get physically out of control.

("Shannon, have you thought about how you'd handle a date who was acting physically inappropriately toward you? I worry about you finding yourself in a situation that you can't control. Perhaps saying something like 'You are making me feel very uncomfortable' or 'I'm not at all ready for this' or 'You have crossed the boundary and I want to go home' would be helpful. Do you have any ideas? Can we practice your favorite line? I have a real fear about possible tough situations and I don't want to see you get hurt or feel scared. Do you understand my concern? Thanks, Shannon. I think you'll handle this well.")

Using this technique also provides us an opportunity to discuss our expectations with our children, while providing them with the skill to fulfill the expectation. Much frustration and even conflict can be caused when children and youth don't know how to carry out their parents' expectations, even if they want to comply.

## Corrective Teaching

This skill helps us respond when our teens do something that we don't like. Corrective teaching is used to stop a problem behavior, give a consequence, and describe the behavior or skill that is desired. The important component in this technique is replacing the problem behavior with a desired behavior, which is more effective than just stopping a negative action. For example:

> "Shannon, I need you to stop walking away from me when I am talking to you. If you can't listen now, then you'll have to come in an hour early tonight and we'll talk then. I realize you are upset, but rather than walk away from me, it's better to just stay and try to talk this problem out. Does that make any sense to you? Can we try to talk with each other? I'd really appreciate talking this through. Thank you for your willingness to try talking this out."

Corrective teaching includes six components:

- Stop the problem behavior.
- Give a consequence for the problem behavior.
- Describe the desired behavior.
- Have them acknowledge what you are saying.
- Practice the desired behavior, if feasible.
- Praise and affirm them.

In corrective teaching, we shouldn't get caught up in the content of an issue—the reasons, explanations and excuses. That's an almost impossible quagmire. We should go right to the behavior that we want to change and the behavior we want to foster. Imagine what corrective teaching would sound like in the following situations:

• Your teen comes home after curfew without calling you.
("Brian, I thought we agreed that you would call if you were going to be late. Since you were an hour late coming in, your curfew will be an hour earlier for next week. I really need you to call if you are going to be late, because I worry if I don't know where you are. Do you understand how I feel about this? OK. Thanks for talking this through.")

• Your teen has alcohol on his/her breath.
("Maggie, I smell alcohol on your breath. We will have to talk more about this tomorrow morning, but know that you'll be grounded. I feel very strongly about teenagers and drinking and I do not accept your drinking. We've talked about ways of avoiding drinking, and we'll talk more about this tomorrow. Do you understand my concerns about this? OK. Thanks for listening and we'll talk tomorrow.")

• Your teen is fighting with his/her siblings.
("Jeff, stop fighting with your brother right now. I think you need to spend some time in your room. If your brother is bothering you, let me handle it, or remove yourself from the situation. You don't have to get in a fight with someone who is much younger than you. Do you understand what I'm saying? Does it make any sense? Now, I appreciate your listening to me. I'll see you in an hour. And as for you...(younger brother)...")

Corrective teaching is a very complex parenting skill because it includes stopping an undesirable behavior and replacing that behavior with a more appropriate behavior. Often this technique is utilized in situations that involve a form of conflict, where tension is present.

Obviously these examples may sound stilted and artificial

and hardly like real life. That's because the emotion is not well portrayed. Therefore, two important points need to be mentioned.

First, when emotions are running high, we should call time out before dealing with the problem. For example, waiting until morning to deal with curfew violations or drinking problems, as in the above examples, may be a better approach than confronting the issue late at night. Calling time out allows the emotions to calm down and also gives us time to think through what we want to say and any possible consequences which may be warranted.

Second, these skills need practice. At first we will stumble through these strategies, but with practice they will become second nature.

## SOME FINAL SUGGESTIONS

The following is a list of practical suggestions for enhancing self-esteem, related to the guidelines for practical parenting in the previous chapter.

1. Call your children or teens by name.
2. Use effective praise (4 to 1 ratio), identifying your children's skills.
3. Teach your children life skills.
4. Listen to your children, looking into their eyes.
5. Comfort them when they need comforting.
6. Ask for and respect their opinions.
7. Accept your children as they are right now.
8. Provide an orderly and stimulating environment.
9. Provide activities that neither bore nor frustrate them.
10. Give them an appropriate level of responsibility.
11. Use positive forms of discipline, practicing corrective teaching.

12. Be consistent.
13. Set reasonable limits on their behavior and explain your expectations. With teenagers, these can be set through mutual discussion.
14. Give your children some control by providing choices.
15. Make promises and follow through.
16. Spend time doing things together.
17. Help your children learn how to get along in a group.

A final reminder: these strategies enable parents to reinforce positive behaviors, to identify new behaviors or skills desired, and to confront negative behaviors and replace them with a more appropriate behavior. Having command of desired behaviors or skills, and knowing when to use them, fosters a child's or teen's sense of being capable. When parents use these skills in a spirit of care and love, then they affirm their children's sense of being loveable. IALAC is at the heart of self-esteem.

# 5 · Fostering Teens' Faith...Roots and Wings

One of the more challenging parental tasks today is passing on faith beliefs and convictions to children. Contrary to when most of us grew up, in today's society faith is an option, not a given. As a child growing up in a Catholic family, I don't remember having any choices about church participation. Going to Mass and attending Catholic schools was a given for me. It's what our family did and I was a willing participant. Not until college did I experience any genuine options concerning religion. Even then, as I searched through my faith and understanding of God, I attended a Catholic college so I was still immersed in the Catholic environment. That upbringing has been a wonderful blessing for me and I suspect that many adults have had a similar experience.

Today, however, regardless of where children go to school, attend religious education programs, or participate in the life of the Church, they are faced with multiple options concerning religion, values, and belief systems. Also, children can't be nor should be "programmed" for faith and religious practice. Faith is ultimately a free response to God's grace, and no one can be forced into that response. That doesn't mean, though, that we have no impact on our children's faith. In fact, we are the primary influence in the faith growth of our children.

This chapter will describe the process of faith development in order to better understand our teenagers' struggle with religion and Church, and will also provide some practical strategies for fostering teens' maturing in faith.

## PROCESS OF FAITH DEVELOPMENT

This phrase indicates that faith develops in individuals in much the same way as one matures psychologically, personally, emotionally, and physically. Faith is a process of growth in relationship with God and God's people and continues to grow and mature throughout our life. However, distinguishing between our relationship with God and our relationship with the community of believers is important. This relationship with the community—the Church—is better understood as religion, the public expression of our relationship with God. Faith is our personal relationship with God. This distinction is important for understanding the faith maturing process in adolescents.

A useful image for understanding this distinction is a person's name. Everyone has a first and last name and each says something different. Our first names identify us as unique individuals with our own characteristics, qualities, hopes, dreams, strengths and weaknesses. First names are signs of our individuality. Faith is similar to first names. Faith is the unique and individual relationship that we have with God. In the Scriptures there are many examples of God calling people by name, and even changing their first names as a sign of that special calling. Abram becomes Abraham,

Simon becomes Peter, Saul becomes Paul, and so on. Faith is
our first name when it comes to relating with God.

We also have a last name, which denotes our belonging to
a family. Families have shared looks, mannerisms, experiences, ways of celebrating, stories and history. All members
are connected in the family, even as they maintain their
identity as individuals. Religion is the last name of our faith
identity. Religion is the family of faith name. I am a Catholic
Christian. I belong to the Catholic family, sharing in the traditions, history, creed, rituals and beliefs of the Catholic
community. One's religious denomination or worshiping
community is one's last name of faith. This image of having
a first and last name is helpful in understanding the process
of faith development in adolescents.


THREE DIMENSIONS OF FAITH

Faith has three important dimensions: believing, trusting,
and doing. Faith is often equated with what a person
believes about God, or with one's personal relationship of
trust in God, or even with how a person acts because of
one's beliefs about and relationship with God. Indeed, faith
is all three. Faith includes these three dimensions of believing, trusting, and doing.

Faith as believing relates to our cognitive or intellectual
capacity. This dimension is the "what" or content of faith:
the creeds, traditions, and beliefs of faith as found in
Church teachings, prayers, and, for Roman Catholics, in the
Catechism. Faith as trusting points toward our personal
relationship with a God who cares for and watches over
each of us. This is the affective dimension of faith anchored
in our feeling personally close to God who is seen as acting
within our life. Finally, faith also has a behavioral dimension in that all people are challenged to live out what they

believe about their relationship with God. Faith as doing God's will includes participation in the worship and activities of the church community, as well as having a compassionate outreach to our neighbors in every arena of our life.

## STYLES OF FAITH

So, how do teens experience and express faith—believing, trusting, and doing—and how does that change throughout their developmental process. Looking back to chapter 2 concerning the developmental tasks during adolescence, parents will find parallels in the faith development of young people. Adolescence was described as a time of testing, questioning, and challenging parents and other authority in order to develop a sense of independence and individuality. Religion is not immune to this process.

Based on the work and scholarship of John Westerhoff, four styles of faith can be described. Westerhoff uses the word "styles," not "stages," in order to avoid seeming judgmental or implying that one stage is better or more mature than another. Westerhoff uses the image of a tree in order to understand how faith develops, each style represented by a ring of the tree.

### Experienced Faith

With the person at the center of the rings, the first style of faith is "experienced faith." Experienced faith is the faith of infants and children. During these early years faith is first experienced primarily through interaction with other "faithing individuals." In experiencing love through their parents, children come to understand that God loves them. In experiencing kindness, forgiveness, security, and acceptance through their parents children come to understand God as a God who is interested in them personally. For children at this age, parents are the most important people in their lives. Children's image of God is commensurate with their image of their parents.

This style is also characterized by children's imitating their parents' behavior, not because they understand it, but because they believe it is important since their parents see it as important. Children will imitate the actions and attitude of their parents in both family and church rituals. Church even has a magical sense, with the stories, prayers, and rituals taking on a special quality for children. In experienced faith, children's experience of trust, love, and acceptance are critical for developing a sense of faith.

### Affiliative Faith

During later childhood and into early adolescence the individual moves into the second style of faith, "affiliative faith." Affiliative faith, as the name implies, is characterized by a sense of belonging. Having experienced a sense of affiliation at home, children and youth now want to join clubs, organizations, and teams. They have a need to belong to church as well. The community of believers provides an identity for our children, their "last name of faith" or their religion. Our children have a need to hear the stories and traditions of this family of faith, they want to participate in the rituals, and they want to act with other members of the faith community. In short, children and youth want to do all the things that other members do. Younger adolescents are copiers. They copy the behaviors, dress, and beliefs of those they admire. They want to belong, reflecting the hunger described in chapter 1. These feelings of belonging and affiliation characterize this style as "religion of the heart." This sense of belonging will become part of their "roots."

## *Searching Faith*

During older adolescence and perhaps into young adulthood, young people developmentally are asserting their individuality. They begin pushing against their parents' rules and limits, questioning everything they once accepted. They are developing their "wings." This pushing and questioning is certainly true also of this "searching style" of faith. If you have ever faced the question, "Why do I have to go to church?" you have experienced this style of faith in your children.

Older teens are searching for meaning in life, that hunger for meaning and purpose, and for values they can call their own, and they are testing what they have been taught. Doubt and critical judgment are necessary during this "religion of the head," for they need to test the community's story and understanding of faith in order to reach convictions of their own. During this time of growth, teens are developing their "first name of faith," their personal understanding and relationship with God. At times teens may seem to have lost their faith because they question their religion's beliefs, rituals, and traditions. A more accurate understanding is to say that in some real sense teens are losing their "religion," even while they are developing their own "faith." In reality, religion is not necessarily lost, as much as placed on the back burner, as teens move from a community understanding of faith to a more personal understanding of faith. Teens often say that they pray best in their own rooms, listening to their music, or while walking in the woods or along a beach. Oftentimes they experience God more personally in creation than they do in a church with other, mostly adult, people.

During this time of development, just as in their psychological development, teens often pull away from their parents, in order to experience a degree of independence. The presence of other caring, trusted adults and young adults in teens' lives who can answer their questions, challenge their reasoning, and provide stability is especially important. This point will be further described in the practical strategies.

## *Owned Faith*

The good news is that when navigated effectively, the searching style of faith leads into "owned faith." Owned faith is the culmination of the process which has been traditionally called "conversion" and characterized by a strength of conviction and belief. From a religion of the heart to one of the head and now to "religion of the will," young adults now have developed a religion that they can call their own, a faith that can be put into action. They struggle to eliminate the gap between belief and actions by committing themselves to a lifestyle in which they really do what they believe. This is a major change in a person's thinking, feeling, willing, and acting. In owned faith, the person's first name and last name of faith are now freely chosen. Faith and religion now make sense, provide meaning and direction, and are deserving of a personal commitment to both God and the community of believers.

A word of caution about the interrelationship of the various styles of faith, however, is necessary. Returning to Westerhoff's image of the tree for depicting the growth in faith, we have to remember that trees don't leave their rings behind as they grow. Likewise in faith development, when a young person seems to be in the searching style of faith, we can't forget that they still need the experience of faith and the sense of belonging provided by the earlier styles. And owned faith doesn't mean that teens (or parents) will not have any more questions. Rather, questioning is the means to further growth in faith, coming to ever deeper understandings of God and the challenge of belonging to a community of believers. The styles are simply a way to better understand faith as a journey throughout one's life, rather than a particular destination. One style is not better or more advanced than another. They overlap, complement each other, and help name the experience of faith one has.

## PRINCIPLES AND STRATEGIES

Throughout this journey of faith, there are practical strategies and experiences that we can utilize to foster this faith maturing process in our children and teens.

### *Practice Our Religion*

The number one influence on the faith of young people is the faith life of their parents. The way we practice our religion is very important. Our participation in Sunday Mass or worship and our involvement in the life of the parish church by participating in retreats, Bible study groups, church organizations and ministries, or adult catechesis sessions are signs to our children that our religion is a significant part of our lives. Parental church involvement grows out of the affiliative style of faith and nurtures parental owned faith. Participation in the church reminds children that belonging to a community of believers is integral to sustaining and expressing faith.

### *Model Our Faith*

In addition to belonging to a worshiping community, we have a great impact on our children's faith when we live our faith in our daily routines and interactions. Faith should influence our lifestyle choices, use of time, how we handle conflicts, the relationships we form, and even how we handle work issues. Perhaps the two most obvious challenges to the impact of faith in real life is how adults drive their car and act at sports events! Do we pray at home in the evening? before family meals? in restaurants? In our prayers do we remember those less fortunate? Do we pray for our teens' intentions? For their friends? Do we model forgiveness and reconciliation in our lives by admitting when we are wrong and not lording it over someone else who has been wrong? How do we handle crises in our life, such as death, divorce, pregnancy, illnesses? Does our faith impact how we celebrate Christmas, Easter, or other holy days? All of these situations are part of life. Our young people watch to see if faith makes sense to us, if faith works for us. Youth are looking for a faith that provides meaning in all areas of their life, and not just on Sundays.

### Talk about Values

Faith has to influence our values. When young people start asking the "why" questions, we should be prepared to answer through the lens of our values and our faith. "Why can't I go drinking? Why should I take school seriously? Why should I abstain from sexual relationships?" These questions, along with the issues of racism and prejudice, justice for others, and a comprehensive approach to "life," are opportunities for parents to express their values, anchoring them in their faith beliefs. Though the temptation is to answer, "Because I said so!" young people really need to hear how we have come to a decision and what values influence our decision-making process. By sharing our stories, concerns, questions, and struggles, and sharing how we worked through these issues, we model faith for our children.

## Connect Children and Teens
## to the Community

Meet teens' hunger for connection by encouraging their participation in the faith community. A sense of belonging is a very strong bond for children. They need the experience of being accepted, welcomed, and supported by the community. Youth need an experience of being able to trust others around them. Parents should encourage youth's participation in appropriate parish activities, including the parish youth ministry programs. Here young people can connect with their peers, creating a positive peer group, and they can also connect with other caring, faith-filled adults. This is an important experience of affiliation. We model this connection through our own involvement in the life of the faith community.

## Doing Faith

One of the most important characteristics of youth spirituality is their need to "do faith." Acting because of one's faith is a powerful experience. Participating in community religious practices like Sunday Mass, a public stations of the cross, a youth retreat, or a public teen pilgrimage offers important opportunities to witness to one's faith. Perhaps the most powerful experience of doing faith is involvement in justice and service projects. Serving in soup kitchens, participating in a work camp, working in shelter programs or community emergency outreach centers, tutoring children, and visiting nursing homes have a very significant impact on teens' faith, responding to their hunger for justice. This experience becomes even more powerful when teens and their parents share the experience together.

*Achieve Religious Literacy*

In addition to the trusting and doing dimensions of faith, we also need to foster youth's believing dimension. Children need to know the traditions, creed, teachings, and stories of the community. They need to know the story of Jesus and the Gospel message. They also need to know what it means to be a Catholic—or whatever their particular denomination. Young people need to know how to participate in the rituals and worship of the Church. Of course, young people need to learn this in a way that is age appropriate, using sound methodology and creative approaches. Youth want to know, even when they are searching and challenging. The faith community needs to be a place where young people can bring their questions and search with others for answers that make sense, meet their needs, and provide meaning and purpose in their lives. We should encourage and support our children's participation in parish religious education programs, youth ministry, and sacramental preparation programs.

We need to remember, however, that education in one's faith is a lifelong process. We need to model, by our own willingness to continue learning about our faith, that there is always a deeper understanding of faith to be gained. In those Catholic dioceses where the sacrament of confirmation is celebrated during the middle or high school years, there is a temptation to consider confirmation as a sacrament of graduation. Parents sometimes portray an attitude that once their children have completed confirmation, they no longer have to participate in religious education because their understanding of faith is complete. Parents are often tempted to bargain with their children, trading off their further attendance at religious education programs for their participation in confirmation. Parish coordinators of religious education and youth ministry are challenged to develop programs that are interesting, relevant, and meaningful, even as we are challenged to encourage our children's ongoing involvement in parish programs.

## *Prayer Experiences*

Young people need to experience prayer as the outpouring of their relationship with a God who cares about them, loves them, and wants to communicate with them. There are two dimensions to prayer, remembering the first name and last name of faith. Youth need to pray in their own language, using their own music and symbols, and in their own space. Many teens say they experience God most often in creation—e.g., at the ocean, in sunsets, or at the mountains, and in their rooms, while listening to their music. During the searching style of faith, young people might say, "Why do I have to go to church to pray? I can pray to God in my own room." This reflects the first name of faith—they are establishing their own personal relationship with God. This dimension needs to be affirmed and supported. Teens really do have to develop their own understanding of God.

The last name of faith, though, is the communal or family name. Young people also belong to a faith community and share that community's understanding of God, their traditions, their rituals, and their ways of praying. Young people should be assisted in understanding and participating in the communal worship. We can greatly influence our teen's experience at Sunday Mass or worship by our own level of participation. If we demonstrate an attitude that our attendance at Mass is solely from obligation, then young people certainly can't be blamed for not wanting to attend. If we are "Christmas and Easter" Christians, attending only on the important holy days, then should we expect anything more from our children? If we race to be the first out of the parking lot after church, how can our children think church is important?

Young people need both personal and communal experiences of prayer. They should be encouraged to pray on their own, in their words, using their music and symbols, and even writing their own prayers and spiritual poems. They should also be encouraged to participate with the faith community in worship experiences. This both/and approach to the personal and communal dimension, the first and last name of faith, fosters young people's relationship with God and deepens their faith.

So, when children say, "Why do I have to go to church?" an appropriate response might be, "Because our family belongs to this church and we have a responsibility as members of the community to pray together with the other members of the church."

## Gathering Experiences

Young people have a hunger for connection; they want and need to belong. Even as they are struggling with their personal identity, they enter into relationships. They join clubs and teams, develop school spirit, follow local sports teams, and join community organizations like scouting, 4-H, volunteer fire departments, and FFA and they like going to concerts. Young people want to be part of something bigger—and this is also true for their faith development. In fact, this desire or hunger to belong is especially important for their faith identity.

In a society that seems to give so many mixed messages about religion, young people find themselves struggling with belonging to a church, or acknowledging participating in church. Coming together with other young people who share the same faith—or at least a similar faith—is very important. These gathering experiences provide much needed support for children's growth in faith.

These gathering experiences begin with the local church youth ministry program. Young people need to gather with their peers right in their own church. They need opportunities to build community with their peers, to feel connected with other "faithing" youth, and to interact with caring, believing adults. Parents should advocate for local youth ministry programs if their church doesn't provide such opportunities.

However, gathering experiences move beyond the local church. Coming together with other young people at diocesan youth rallies, regional youth events, and national youth conferences gives youth a sense of belonging to something bigger. In 1997, 17,000 young people attended the National Catholic Youth Conference in Kansas City, Missouri. In 1993, 400,000 Catholic young people traveled to Denver, Colorado for World Youth Day with Pope John Paul II. One of the main benefits of this event, which is conducted every other year, was youth's connection with their peers from around the world. Truly, they felt that they belonged to something bigger and something universal, and this experience of church continues to provide support and encouragement for those young people in attendance.

Gathering experiences are communal events, creating a sense of belonging to the family of faith, and fostering their "last name" of faith. However, these experiences also foster youth's personal journey of faith—their "first name" of faith. Gathering experiences provide youth with the opportunity to clarify and celebrate their personal faith, even as they experience belonging to something bigger than themselves.

## Scriptures of Their Own Lives

Young people are searching for a personal understanding of God, their first name of faith, reflecting their hunger for the holy. As they do so, they must be able and encouraged to look for God's presence in their personal, lived experiences. Young people should be assisted in naming their experiences of a God who is active and present in their lives. God does not wait to be invited into the lives of young people. God takes the initiative and is present, but waits to be identified or named. Many young people need the language to help them understand and express their experiences of God.

Parents, and other caring, faith-filled adults, can assist young people in experiencing God's presence in their joys and sorrows, their hopes and dreams, and in their day to day life. Of course this requires that we have the language to name the presence of God in our own lives! We can ask our teenagers where they experience God, where they pray best, where they feel joy and sorrow, for God is present there. And we can share our experiences. The following are sample questions that parents can use with teenagers with regard to faith and religion.

- Where do you most experience the presence of God?
- Where do you pray best? When do you pray?
- What is the best part of belonging to our parish? What is the one thing you would change about our parish?
- On a scale of 1 to 10, how important is going to Mass on Sunday for you? What makes it a ____ (2, 5, 7, etc.)?
- Have you ever had an experience where your faith was really tested?
- Have you ever had an experience where your faith has really helped you?
- What most confuses you about faith and God?
- What Church teaching most confuses you?

- How is your faith different now from when you were in grade school?
- What experiences, places, or persons have really fostered your growth in faith?

Parents can develop more questions as they speak with their teenagers about faith and religion. This faith-sharing is a very important task because young people will never understand the Hebrew-Christian scriptures until they can read the scriptures of their own lives. Therein, young people experience the God who is always active and present. And we should be open to having our own understanding of God challenged and perhaps deepened by our teenagers' experience of God. Young people often have very powerful experiences of God, and they can enrich our faith, if there is a relationship that enables them to share these experiences with us.

### Power of Good Memories

As stated earlier, one of my favorite posters says, "There are only two things we can give our children that last: the first is wings and the second is roots." Many young people move through the searching style of faith, challenging the beliefs and practices of their parents and their church, and some even move away from regular participation and association with the institutional church. This is a time of "wings" for youth, a time for stretching and flying and experimenting—not only in terms of faith, but also in terms of finding themselves, deciding on their important values, entering into relationships, and making decisions about their future. And though all of these processes seem to take young people away from home, parents, and church, if we have provided an anchor, if we have provided "roots," then their flying is not nearly so frightening for our children, or for us.

These roots are established first in the family, in their relationship with us. Teens will remember the care, concern, and support they have experienced at home. They will remember the freedom to ask hard questions and to have different answers than their parents. They will remember how their questions and differing opinions were listened to respectfully, even as they heard their parents' beliefs and faith stories.

Roots are also teens' memories of caring, believing adult role models who expressed love and concern for them and their memory of a welcoming and supportive community of believers who invited them into their midst and encouraged their active participation. Roots are youth's memory of those times when they experienced God because others were visible signs of God's love for them.

The memories that young people have of belonging to a worshiping community, of putting their faith in action through service to others, of praying at home and with their church, of gathering with their peers in shared faith experiences—such memories are powerful. These memories will sustain young people as they deal with the sometimes harsh realities of life and as they struggle to develop their "last name of faith." These memories, these roots, give young people something to come back home to.

# Conclusion

An important caution to acknowledge is that implementing all of the suggestions and strategies described in the previous chapters does not guarantee a perfect relationship between parents and their teenagers. There will always be problems, tensions, and conflicts. We will make mistakes, and our children will make mistakes as well. We will get frustrated, even angry with our children. And they, in return, will be distant and withdrawn at times. But if we act out of love, if we clearly speak of the affection we feel for each member of our family, then we will survive the rough times. Skills will never substitute for a lack of love in our families, but good parenting skills will provide more avenues to express the love we feel for our children and teenagers.

We have to keep perspective, looking at our long-term relationship with our children. We have to remember that someday we will be friends with our children. As our children grow older, more mature, and more independent, we need to affirm them for who they are and for who they are becoming. Indeed, our children and teenagers will be a blessing to us, and that will make all our efforts worthwhile.

# Appendix

Exercise 1: Ten Ways To Get Along With Parents (as developed by Shannon McCarty, the author's daughter)

1.  **Treat them as you want them to treat you.** Even though it sounds pretty basic, if teenagers want to be treated with respect and fairness, then we have to treat our parents the same way.

2.  **Remember, parents are people too.** That means they are human, they make mistakes, they lose their temper, they say things they don't necessarily mean. And they want to do their best, especially in raising their children.

3.  **Handle the ordinary, and the special will take care of itself.** If we handle our normal curfews, chores, and school responsibilities, when something special comes up, we have a better chance to have the rules relaxed.

4.  **It's OK to call timeout during family arguments.** If you or your parents get really emotional during argu-

ments—and that's when we say things we don't really mean—then agree to call timeout, and come back to the issue when everyone has cooled down.

5. **At least once a day, talk to your parents.** Communication begins with a willingness to just talk. Parents get nervous when they feel out of touch with their children. So each day, just talk to them about things going on at school, or with your friends, or at your church group.

6. **Plan escape routes.** Everyone gets into difficult situations, whether on a date, at a party, or just out with friends. So think about your options, in case something happens. It's a sign of responsibility that we can handle ourselves.

7. **Agree on the basics.** Talk with your parents about curfews, school expectations, household chores, driving with friends, and other issues, rather than relying on mind-reading. Perhaps you can renegotiate the basics on your birthday, so as you get older, you gain more rights and responsibilities.

8. **Tell your parents that they are doing a good job.** Parents get very little training on how to be good parents. It's more like trial and error. You will really surprise them by telling them they are doing OK.

9. **Try to become friends with your parents.** As strange as it sounds, when we get older we will be friends with our parents. So begin being friendly, talking with them, and sharing some time together.

10. **Learn how to say "I'm sorry."** It's a sign of maturity to admit when we are wrong about something or at fault. Also, we have a better chance of convincing our parents when we are right.

**Exercise 2: Survey on Parent–Teen Relationships**

This exercise should be completed by parents and their teenagers separately; then they can compare their responses.

**For teenagers:**

**Yes No**

\_\_ \_\_   1. Do your parents wait until you are through talking before having their say?

\_\_ \_\_   2. Does your family do things as a group?

\_\_ \_\_   3. Do your parents respect your opinions?

\_\_ \_\_   4. Do your parents tend to lecture too much?

\_\_ \_\_   5. Do you discuss your personal problems with either of your parents?

\_\_ \_\_   6. Do your parents talk to you as if you were much younger than you are?

\_\_ \_\_   7. Do your parents show interest in your activities?

\_\_ \_\_   8. Do you and either parent discuss matters of sex?

\_\_ \_\_   9. Do your parents trust you?

\_\_ \_\_ 10. Do you find it hard to share how you feel at home?

\_\_ \_\_ 11. Do your parents have confidence in your abilities?

\_\_ \_\_ 12. Do your parents consider your ideas before making decisions affecting you?

__ __ 13. Do your parents explain their reasons for the decisions they make regarding you?

__ __ 14. Do you and your parents try to see one another's side of things?

__ __ 15. Do you help your parents understand you by telling them how you think and feel?

Bonus: In light of your answers to the questions above, rate your relationship with your parents.

_____very good    _____good    _____fair    _____poor

Bonus: Think of three constructive ideas on how to improve your relationship with your parents. Write them here.

**For parents:**

**Yes No**

__ __ 1. Do your teenagers wait until you are through talking before having their  say?

__ __ 2. Does your family do things as a group?

__ __ 3. Do your teenagers respect your opinions?

__ __ 4. Do you tend to lecture your teenagers too much?

__ __ 5. Do your teenagers discuss their personal problems with either parent?

__ __ 6. Do you find yourself talking to your teenagers as if they were much younger than they really are?

__ __ 7. Do your teenagers show much interest in your activities?

\_\_ \_\_ 8. Do your teenagers discuss matters of sex with either parent?

\_\_ \_\_ 9. Do you trust your teenagers?

\_\_ \_\_ 10. Do your teenagers share how they feel at home?

\_\_ \_\_ 11. Do you have confidence in your teenagers' abilities?

\_\_ \_\_ 12. Do you consider your teenagers' ideas when making decisions affecting them?

\_\_ \_\_ 13. Do you explain your reasons for the decisions you make regarding them?

\_\_ \_\_ 14. Do you and your teenagers try to see one another's side of things?

\_\_ \_\_ 15. Do your teenagers help you understand them by telling you how they think and feel?

Bonus: In light of your answers to the questions above, rate your relationship with your teenagers.

\_\_\_\_\_very good   \_\_\_\_\_good   \_\_\_\_\_fair   \_\_\_\_\_poor

Bonus: Think of three constructive ideas on how to improve your relationship with your teenagers. Write them here.

**Exercise 3: The ABCs of Showing Love** (Adapted from Group Publishing, Inc.)

This exercise can be completed by both teenagers and parents and then the responses shared. When two parents are completing this exercise, they should do it separately before sharing their responses.

**For teenagers:**

Below are many different ways of showing love to parents. Rate yourself on how often you show love in these ways. (O = often; S = sometimes; H = hardly ever; N = never).

\_\_\_ I ask my parents how I can help.
\_\_\_ I give my parents flowers.
\_\_\_ I try to understand my parents' viewpoint.
\_\_\_ I thank my parents for their help.
\_\_\_ I talk to my parents about things that interest them.
\_\_\_ I do fun things with my parents.
\_\_\_ I listen to my parents.
\_\_\_ I tell my parents that I love them.
\_\_\_ I send notes or cards to my parents, on more than birthdays.
\_\_\_ I spend special time alone with Mom or Dad.
\_\_\_ I pray for my parents.
\_\_\_ I let my parents know they are special to me.
\_\_\_ I speak to my parents with respect.
\_\_\_ I tell my parents I appreciate them.
\_\_\_ I hug my Mom or Dad.
\_\_\_ I thank my parents for supporting our family.
\_\_\_ I forgive my parents when they make a mistake.
\_\_\_ I celebrate special times with my parents.
\_\_\_ I obey the rules my parents set.
\_\_\_ I spend time doing things with my parents because I want to.

Now score yourself according to how many ways you checked O or S.

• **14 to 20**–Bravo! You really know how to let your parents know you care! Keep it up!
• **7 to 14**–Good work! It sounds as if you know how to show love to your parents. But you could stand to do it more often or in a greater variety of ways. Try three new ways this week.
• **0 to 6**–Ouch! You need to work on showing love more. Pick out two new ways to show love each week for the next three weeks, and give them a try. Find ways that are comfortable for you, and meaningful to you and your parents.

**For parents:**

Below are many different ways of showing love to your teenagers. Rate yourself on how often you show love in these ways. (O=often; S=sometimes; H=hardly ever; N=never).

\_\_\_ I ask my teenagers how I can help them.
\_\_\_ I give my teenagers flowers.
\_\_\_ I try to understand my teenagers' viewpoint.
\_\_\_ I thank my teenagers for their help.
\_\_\_ I talk to my teenagers about things that interest them.
\_\_\_ I do fun things with my teenagers.
\_\_\_ I listen to my teenagers.
\_\_\_ I tell my teenagers that I love them.
\_\_\_ I send notes or cards to my teenagers, on more than birthdays.
\_\_\_ I spend special time alone with each of my teenagers.
\_\_\_ I pray for my teenagers.
\_\_\_ I let my teenagers know they are special to me.
\_\_\_ I tell my teenagers that I appreciate them.
\_\_\_ I hug my teenagers.

\_\_\_ I thank my teenagers for their contributions to our family.

\_\_\_ I forgive my teenagers when they make a mistake.

\_\_\_ I talk to my teenagers about the rules we set for them.

\_\_\_ I spend time doing things with my teenagers because I want to.

Now score yourself according to how many times you checked O or S.

• **14 to 20**–Bravo! You really know how to let your teenagers know you care! Keep it up!

• **7 to 13**–Good work! It sounds as if you know how to show love to your teenagers. But you could stand to do it more often or in a greater variety of ways. Try three new ways this week.

• **0 to 6**–Ouch! You need to work on showing love more. Pick out two new ways to show love each week for the next three weeks, and give them a try. Find ways that are comfortable for you, and meaningful to you and your teenagers.

**Exercise 4: Parent–Teen Conflict Resolution**

Conflict is a part of every close human relationship. When resolved respectfully, conflict is actually healthy because it promotes communication and yields solutions which work for everyone. Working at resolving conflict also communicates to your teenagers that you take them seriously and respect their feelings and opinions. Conflict involves two important dimensions: feelings and content or the issue causing the conflict. Successful resolution fosters a ventilating of the feelings and a discussion of the issue. The following suggestions will help you to "fight fair" as you work through conflict with your teenagers.

## Rules for Fighting Fair

1. Realize that your teenagers are no longer children and therefore they are capable of reasoning in a more adult way. So, start by stating your belief that together you and your teen can resolve the problem.

2. Ask non-blaming questions to clarify the issue. An important step is spending time in naming or identifying the real issue.

3. Listen to your teen's point of view and realize that we all see things differently.

4. Share your feelings honestly about the issue, and encourage your teenagers to express their feelings, but watch for "fouls."

5. Stick to the issue. Don't dredge up past hurts or problems.

6. When you have been wrong, admit it. Ask for forgiveness.

7. Be willing to explore compromises. Avoid a win-lose resolution, which creates negative feelings and really doesn't create an effective resolution.

8. Don't give up until you have come to some resolution.

9. Set a time to discuss how the resolution is going and to see if it needs revisiting.

## Fouls Which Block the Process

| | | |
|---|---|---|
| Name calling | Blaming | Physical violence |
| Yelling | Threatening | Obscenities |
| Rolling Eyes | Insults | Using the "Silent Treatment" |

**Exercise 5: Don't Say...Do Say!**

This exercise enables parents to identify sentences and statements which either hinder ("Don't Say") or foster ("Do Say") effective relationships. Circle any you have used in conversation with your teenagers. After you are finished, ask your teenager(s) to star those they have heard. Compare your lists and share your reactions.

Don't say...

"As long as you are under my roof..."
"Your room is such a mess. How can you live like that?"
"Haven't you finished your homework yet?"
"Who was **that** on the phone?"
"Go ask your father (mother)."
"You're the oldest and should be more responsible."
"Money doesn't grow on trees."
"Good things don't come easy."
"When I was your age..."
"You are old enough to know better."
"That's what you get for waiting until the last moment."
"Because I said so."  ·
"I don't need a reason."
"I love you, but..."
"What's wrong with teenagers today?"

Do Say...

"Because we are a family..."
"I love you."
"You are doing a good job of growing up."
"I believe in you."
"That sounds like a difficult decision you have to make."
"I really like your friends."
"I liked the way you handled..."

"You do a good job of budgeting your time."
"You are really helpful around the house."
"You make good decisions."
"You look very nice today."
"I appreciate your going to church with us. I know it's not easy at times."
"Thank you."
"I am proud of you."
"I don't understand...can you help me?"

**Exercise 6: Youth–Parent Questionnaires** (from "Helping You Decide"by the National Association of State Boards of Education, 1986)

Parents and teenagers should fill out their respective questionnaires separately and then share their responses.

**Youth Questionnaire:**

1. I spend about_____hours a week talking with my (mother) (father).

2. When something is bothering me, my (mother) (father) usually: (check the one that comes closest)
    a. assumes my problems can't be all that serious.
    b. figures it out before I say anything.
    c. is willing to take the time to listen.
    d. goes overboard and lectures me. I know (she) (he) means well but it never helps.

3. When I ask permission to do something, my (mother) (father):
    a. usually says "yes" because (she) (he) trusts me.
    b. usually says "yes," but I wonder if (she) (he) is even listening.
    c. questions me and sometimes really invades my privacy.
    d. usually says "no" because (she) (he) doesn't trust me.
    e. other_____

4. My best friends are: (list names)

    _____
    _____
    _____
    _____

5. My most frustrating experience of the past few weeks
   was:_____

   _____
   _____

6. My most frustrating experience with my (mother)
   (father) in the past few weeks was:_____

   _____
   _____

7. One of the things about me that makes my (mother)
   (father) feel proud is:_____

   _____
   _____

8. One of the things that bothers my (mother) (father)
   about me is:_____

   _____
   _____

9. The biggest decision I have ever made on my own is:

   _____
   _____

10. A mutually agreeable decision that my (mother) (father)
    and I have made together within the last month is:

   _____
   _____

**Parent Questionnaire:**

1. Right now, I spend about_____hours a week talking with
   my (son) (daughter).

2. When something is bothering (him) (her) I usually:
   (check the one that comes the closest).
   a. assume that the problem can't be all that serious.

   b. am sensitive to the fact that there is a problem—and I am often right about that.
   c. take the time to listen.
   d. become deeply involved—giving freely of my experience and advice.

3. When my (son) (daughter) asks for permission to do something, I: (check the one that comes closest)
   a. usually say "yes" because I trust (him) (her).
   b. usually say "yes" because (he) (she) is going to do it anyway.
   c. want more information and may want to check things out for myself.
   d. usually say "no" because (he) (she) has such a poor track record.
   e. other_____

4. My (son's) (daughter's) best friends are: (list names)

   _____
   _____
   _____
   _____

5. (His) (Her) most frustrating experience of the past few weeks was:_____

_____
_____

6. The most frustrating experience (he) (she) had **with me** in the past few weeks was:_____

_____
_____

7. One thing about my (son) (daughter) that I am proud of is:_____

_____
_____

8. One thing that bothers me about (him) (her) is:_____

_____

_____

9. The biggest decision my (son) (daughter) has ever made on (his) (her) own is:_____

_____

_____

10. A mutually agreeable decision that my (son) (daughter) and I have made together within the last month is:_____

_____

_____

**Exercise 7: I Think We'd Get Along Better If...** (From Audrey Taylor in "Network.") After completing the appropriate reflection sheet, parents and teenagers compare their responses.

**Teenage Letter:**

Dear Parent:

As your teenager, I think we'd get along better if you would: (circle your 7 favorite "advices")

1. Admit it when you're wrong.
2. Spend some time with me one-on-one.
3. Listen to me. Really listen to me. Don't lecture me.
4. Don't compare me to my brothers and sisters.
5. Don't say, "When I was your age..."
6. Trust me more. And don't always give me the third degree when I want to go somewhere with my friends.
7. Appreciate me more. Say "thank you" more often instead of taking me for granted.
8. Stop bugging me about grades and studying.
9. Allow me my privacy. Don't listen in on my phone conversations, check my mail...
10. Laugh more.
11. Stop complaining about my music.
12. Compliment me more. Give me some praise once in a while.
13. Don't compare me to other teenagers.
14. Tell me about sex and how to handle it.
15. Stay home more often.
16. Pray more...for me and with me.
17. Watch TV less.
18. Spend less time on work and more time on the family.

**Parent Letter:**

Dear Teenager:

As your parent, I think we'd get along better if you would: (circle your 7 favorite "advices")

1. Admit it when you are wrong.
2. Stay home more often.
3. Listen to me. Really listen to me. Don't turn me off.
4. Care more about your brothers and sisters. Fight less.
5. Don't say, "You just don't understand me."
6. Be worthy of my trust. Don't lie to me.
7. Appreciate me more. Say "thank you" more often instead of just taking me for granted.
8. Put more effort into your grades and studying.
9. Don't overdo your privacy. Come out of your room and share with the family once in a while.
10. Laugh more.
11. Turn down the volume on your music.
12. Compliment me more. Give me some praise once in a while.
13. Don't compare me to other parents.
14. Ask me more about sex and how to handle it.
15. Stay home more often.
16. Pray more...for me and with me.
17. Watch TV less.
18. Clean up your room.

**Exercise 8: Trustworthiness** (adapted from GROUP publishing)

Parents and teenagers should complete their respective exercises and then compare responses and scores.

**For teenagers:**

How trustworthy are you? Circle the appropriate number for each of the following areas. Then add the numbers and read the scoring table to see what your score means.

1. How often do you come home by curfew?

    | Always | | Sometimes | | Never |
    |---|---|---|---|---|
    | 1 | 2 | 3 | 4 | 5 |

2. How often do you do all your chores on time?

    | Always | | Sometimes | | Never |
    |---|---|---|---|---|
    | 1 | 2 | 3 | 4 | 5 |

3. How often do you do all the homework you're supposed to?

    | Always | | Sometimes | | Never |
    |---|---|---|---|---|
    | 1 | 2 | 3 | 4 | 5 |

4. How often do you let parents know your plans?

    | Always | | Sometimes | | Never |
    |---|---|---|---|---|
    | 1 | 2 | 3 | 4 | 5 |

5. How often are you careful as a driver (or as a passenger with other teen drivers)?

    | Always | | Sometimes | | Never |
    |---|---|---|---|---|
    | 1 | 2 | 3 | 4 | 5 |

6. How often do you lie to your parents?

    | Always | | Sometimes | | Never |
    |---|---|---|---|---|
    | 5 | 4 | 3 | 2 | 1 |

Total Points:_____

Scoring:

**6 to 10**   Congratulations! You deserve to be trusted.

**11 to 15**   You know how to be trustworthy–keep up the good work.

**16 to 24**   You have some work to do. Try to be more consistent in your responsibilities.

**25 to 30**   Do you wonder why your parents don't trust you? Start being more responsible and give them a reason to trust you.

**For parents:**

How is the level of trust and communication in your relationship with your teenager? Circle the appropriate number for each of the following areas. Then add the numbers and read the scoring table to see what the score means.

1. How often do you reward your teen's responsibility by extending curfew or other freedoms?

| Always | | Sometimes | | Never |
|---|---|---|---|---|
| 1 | 2 | 3 | 4 | 5 |

2. How often do you respect your teen's privacy? (Their room, letters, diaries, phone calls)

| Always | | Sometimes | | Never |
|---|---|---|---|---|
| 1 | 2 | 3 | 4 | 5 |

3. How often do you show interest in your teen's school and other activities?

| Always | | Sometimes | | Never |
|---|---|---|---|---|
| 1 | 2 | 3 | 4 | 5 |

4. Do you know your teen's friends and their leisure time plans?

| Always | | Sometimes | | Never |
|---|---|---|---|---|
| 1 | 2 | 3 | 4 | 5 |

5. With clear expectations, how often do you allow your teen to borrow the car (or drive the car with you along)?

| Always | | Sometimes | | Never |
|--------|---|-----------|---|-------|
| 1 | 2 | 3 | 4 | 5 |

6. How often do you share your real feelings with your teen (have you ever said "I'm sorry" or "I'm wrong")?

| Always | | Sometimes | | Never |
|--------|---|-----------|---|-------|
| 1 | 2 | 3 | 4 | 5 |

Total Points:_____

Scoring:

**6 to 10**    Congratulations! You're working hard at your relationship!

**11 to 15**    You are on the way; keep up the good work.

**16 to 24**    It would be good to work on communication in your family.

**25 to 30**    Communication and trust are a real issue in your family.

## Exercise 9: Dinner Table Discussion

The following questions can be used as conversation starters. Parents should not take on the "authority" or "expert" role or dominate the conversation. These questions are stated in a general way: referring to "teenagers" and "their parents" rather than "you" and "in our family." Keeping the discussion general makes it less threatening and less personal and may initially foster a better discussion. Once the family is comfortable discussing various issues, the questions can be focused on their family, their teenagers, and their parents. Parents and teenagers are encouraged to create their own questions. Perhaps the family could designate one night each week as "Bring a Question Night" or "Hot Topic Night."

1. What are the three key issues, concerns, or problems facing teenagers today? What creates stress for teenagers? What are the issues for adults? What creates stress for parents today?

2. What are the biggest sources of conflict at home for teenagers or with their parents?

3. What one thing could parents do to get along better with their teenagers? What one thing could teenagers do to get along better with their parents?

4. What do teenagers need from their parents today, in order to face all the pressures of growing up?

5. What causes all the pressure for teenagers to drink alcohol today? Was there the same pressure when parents were teenagers? What do some teenagers do to avoid the drinking, while still attending parties where drinking occurs?

6. What is causing teenagers to engage in drug use today? What are the most popular drugs used in our neighborhood? How extensive is drug use in the schools? What was drug use like when the parents were teenagers? How can a teenager say "no" to drugs without looking "weird"?

7. Where do teenagers get most of their information about sex? What message does the media (TV shows, movies, advertisements) give about sexual relationships? Is there pressure today for teenagers to have sex? Where did parents get their information about sex when they were teenagers? Do teenagers today ever have "the talk" with their parents?

8. What qualities do teenagers look for in a relationship? What kind of person do they want to date? What is the "ideal date"? What was the "ideal date" when parents were teenagers?

9. Is peer pressure as strong as the media says it is? What gives peer pressure such power to control behavior? How do teenagers handle peer pressure? What was peer pressure like when the parents were teens? What behaviors does/did peer pressure encourage?

10. How many teenagers go to church or are involved in church activities? What do teenagers like about their church? What don't teenagers like about their church? What changes would churches have to make in order to attract teenagers? When parents were teenagers did they go to church?

11. How would teenagers describe God? Where do teenagers pray best? When do teenagers most experience God's presence? What do teenagers think about

Jesus? When parents were teenagers, how did they describe God? When did they pray? When do they pray now? How important is faith today?

12. What do teenagers like most about their school? Like least about their school? Who are the best teachers and what makes them the best? What are the favorite subjects? Worst subjects? What are the best extracurricular activities, organizations, and clubs?

13. What do teenagers think the world will be like in five years? ten years? twenty-five years? What do teenagers most look forward to? Least look forward to? What is the best thing about becoming an adult? What is the worst thing about becoming an adult? When parents were teenagers, what did they think the future would be like?

14. Local current events: What do you think of the level of _____ (violence, poverty, homelessness, drug abuse, environmental pollution, etc.) in our country (city, community, neighborhood)? What seem to be the causes? What should our government do? What should the common citizens do? What were the issues when parents were teenagers?

15. International current events: What do you make of the situation in_____? What do you think is the issue? What should our government do? What were the international issues when parents were teenagers?

**Exercise 10: Making Good Decisions:**
**The DECIDE Approach**

Decision making is one of the most critical skills for young people to develop. Described here is a step by step process for responsible decision making which can be applied to situations confronting our teenagers.

**D ·** **Define** the issue, question or problem. Gather the facts about the situation and clearly name the decision to be made.

**E ·** **Explore** the options and alternatives. Look at the various choices that will solve the problem.

**C ·** **Consider** the consequences of each alternative. Consider the pros and cons, the advantages and disadvantages of each of the alternatives.

**I ·** **Inquire** about others' opinions. Ask parents or other significant adults for their advice. Consider your personal values and morals, your faith stance, your Church's teachings, and society's understanding of acceptable behavior.

**D ·** **Decide** on the best course of action. Having considered all the facts, alternatives, consequences, and others' input, make the decision.

**E ·** **Evaluate** your decision after having acted on it. Evaluate the consequences and make any necessary changes and modifications.

Two important concepts for decision making:

**Responsible decision making** refers to making decisions

only after carefully considering the possible alternatives and consequences.

**Accountability** refers to accepting the responsibility for the consequences of one's decisions. This includes the praise and congratulations when good decisions are made, as well as the results of poor decisions.